Tahoe

From Timber Barons
to Ecologists

Douglas H. Strong

University of Nebraska Press
Lincoln and London

Library of Congress Cataloging-in-Publication Data
Strong, Douglas Hillman.
Tahoe : from timber barons to ecologists /
Douglas H. Strong.
p.   cm.
Includes bibliographical references and index.
ISBN 0-8032-9258-9 (pbk. : alk. paper)
1. Regional planning – Tahoe, Lake, Region
(Calif. and Nev.) – History.   2. Nature – Effect of
human beings on – Tahoe, Lake, Region (Calif. and Nev.)
3. Environmental protection – Tahoe, Lake, Region
(Calif. and Nev.) – History.   4. Tahoe, Lake,
Region (Calif. and Nev.) – History.   I. Title.
HT392.5.T3S79   1999
333.7'09794'38 – dc21   98-36172
CIP

*Dedicated to all Tahoans
who have worked so diligently
to restore the ecological health
of the Tahoe Basin*

Contents

Illustrations

Photographs

Maps

Preface

Lake Tahoe is breathtaking. Millions of visitors each year marvel at its crystal blue water. The lake's fame has spread worldwide, attracting tourists, permanent residents, and commercial development. An unexpected consequence has been environmental deterioration, even of the quality of Tahoe's immense volume of water.

Ever since the first settlers arrived, people have quarreled over who should control the land and resources within the Tahoe Basin. Local residents and outside investors have favored private ownership of property and "free enterprise." They have argued that the Tahoe Basin belongs to those with title to the land and that legal owners should be free to use the land as they see fit, whether this means cutting its timber or building a high-rise casino-hotel. The resulting deforestation and urbanization have not pleased everyone. Even in the early days of settlement, a few individuals argued that the priceless heritage of Tahoe belonged to all people. They insisted that major portions of the basin should be set aside in parks or forest reserves. Others promoted a middle ground, advocating controlled growth that they hoped would allow economic development without incurring high environmental costs or loss of scenic amenities.

Tahoe's environmental problems challenge even people with the best of intentions. Soil erosion, air pollution, and deteriorating water quality threaten its fragile environment. In addition, social problems such as traffic congestion, rising crime rates, and a shortage of middle- and low-income housing have proliferated. As Charles

Goldman, an expert on the water quality of the lake, stated, "In a sense Tahoe represents in microcosm the environmental problems of the twentieth century, both on a national and international basis."[1] Goldman minced no words in describing the condition of the lake: "Lake Tahoe is being polluted. . . . If the pollution of Lake Tahoe is not stopped now, the pollutants will continue to accumulate in the lake, and in time the lake will turn from clear blue to turbid green."[2]

I share Goldman's concern for the future of Tahoe because I witnessed its transformation from a sleepy mountain backwater in the late 1930s to the rapidly growing year-round recreational and urban area it is today. As a child I lost my way in the forest near Stateline on the south shore but was rescued by a friendly cabin owner and the local sheriff. In the same area today it would be hard to find a grove of trees large enough in which to hide.

The following story of Tahoe's transformation is based largely on my out-of-print book, *Tahoe: An Environmental History* (University of Nebraska Press, 1984). This study provided a documented account of how human settlement affected the Tahoe Basin and how citizens and government attempted to solve the environmental problems that resulted. The current revision contains limited documentation; notes are restricted almost entirely to direct quotations. I hope that *Tahoe: From Timber Barons to Ecologists*, shorter and updated, will reach an increasing number of people who appreciate Tahoe's beauty and desire to help protect its special environmental qualities.

Space does not permit mention of everyone who assisted me in the course of this study, both in the original research and the revised update. Librarians and archivists gave unstintingly of their time. Scholars, planners, and informed citizens answered numerous questions. These include Donald J. Pisani, Joseph H. Engbeck, David Beesley, Thomas R. Cox, Barbara Lekisch, Andrew R. Schmidt, Glenn S. Smith, Sari Sommarstrom, Kenneth C. and Lynne Smith, Bob Harris, Jim Baetge, Dennis T. Machida, Ray Lacey, Robert McDowell, Don Lane, R. J. Nicolle, Jim Hildinger, Rochelle Nason, Steve Chilton, Steve Teshara, Cindy M. Gustafson, J. Dennis Crabb,

Susan E. Scholley, Jeffrey P. Zippin, Susan Lindström, and Leo Poppoff. Any errors are solely my responsibility. My thanks to my daughter Beret E. Strong for her thoughtful editing. The book's dedication reflects my respect for all those who care about the future of the Lake Tahoe Basin.

Tahoe

1   From Pioneers to Urbanites

Tahoe's Natural History

The striking beauty of Lake Tahoe resulted from millions of years of geologic changes. The Sierra Nevada, in which Tahoe is nestled, extends more than 400 miles from near Lassen Peak in the north to Tehachapi Pass in the south. Its eastern edge forms a tremendous fault scarp that proved a formidable barrier to east-west travel, especially in the days of horse and wagon. To the west, the Sierra slopes gradually toward California's Central Valley. The Tahoe Basin, underlain primarily with granitic rock, resulted from faults that allowed it to drop, forming what is called a graben or trough. The graben rests between two crests of the Sierra Nevada—the main crest to the west and the Carson Range to the east. Additional uplifting and volcanic activity have altered the landscape.

Within the past two million years, extensive glaciation and deposition further transformed the topography. Sheets of ice more than a thousand feet thick covered mountain valleys and all but the highest peaks on the western side of the basin. The ice scoured out cirques and steep slopes as well as the basins below, where Fallen Leaf Lake, Cascade Lake, Emerald Bay, and smaller lakes and ponds formed. The fragments of rock and silt carried by the ice and water eventually came to rest in moraines; one of these can be seen just east of the present Lake Tahoe airport. Because of the "rain shadow" cast by the main crest of the Sierra, the Carson Range to the east held only small glaciers, if any, on the shaded sides of the peaks and so remains relatively gentle and rolling in contrast to the highly sculptured peaks to the west of the lake.

At the north end of the basin, large streams of ice descended from Squaw Valley and neighboring valleys to block the Truckee River canyon (the outlet of Lake Tahoe), forming an ice dam that at one time raised the water level of the lake several hundred feet above its current depth. When this and other ice dams formed by glacial advances gave way, great granite boulders hurtled downstream with the floodwaters and came to rest beyond the present-day site of Reno. At other times the level of the lake fluctuated several hundred feet because volcanic flows of basalt blocked the outlet, only to erode gradually away. Today andesitic mudflows and lava form a natural dam at the outlet of the lake, 6,223 feet above sea level, at Tahoe City. Even so, the "surface elevation of Lake Tahoe has stood considerably lower than the present for long periods of time."[1]

With the end of the glacial epoch more than ten thousand years ago, silt and sand from the melting glaciers eroded rapidly, depositing layer after layer of sediment on the relatively flat lake bottom. Sediment collecting at the edge of the lake formed deltas, the largest of which is now the site of the city of South Lake Tahoe. The potential for erosion in the basin has remained high because the soil tends to be shallow and coarse, lacking humus and other material that hold moisture and bind the soil together. The processes of erosion and deposition continue inevitably as the Sierra wears down, particularly where decomposed granite is exposed to running water.

The Lake Tahoe Basin, formed by these geologic forces and defined as the land and water area that contributes to the outflow from the lake, is small—slightly more than 500 square miles of land and water. Most of the terrain in the basin is quite steep. Land development in recent years has therefore been concentrated on the more level land along the lakeshore, especially at the southern end of the basin. The perimeter of the basin is rugged, particularly in the Desolation Wilderness to the west, and is relatively unaffected by human contact.

Tahoe itself is exceptionally deep (1,645 feet), exceeded in depth by only a few lakes in the world, including Crater Lake in Oregon. Its water is perpetually in motion; the surface never freezes except occasionally on the fringes. Because of its depth and size (22 miles long and 12 miles wide), Tahoe holds an immense volume of water; unleashed, it would flood the state of California to a depth of more than 14 inches. Simply to refill the lake with the natural inflow would take about seven hundred years. The lake's outlet, the Truckee River, never reaches the ocean; much of Tahoe's water evaporates, and the remainder flows into landlocked Pyramid Lake and irrigation canals in Nevada.

Most of Tahoe's water arrives via storms originating in the northern Pacific Ocean and bearing moist marine air that drops heavy loads of snow during the winter months, especially at higher elevations. Winter temperatures are moderate, especially near the lake, seldom dropping below 0 degrees Fahrenheit for any length of time. During the spring thaw, the melting snow feeds more than sixty inlets to the lake, primarily on the wetter western side of the basin. Summers, on the other hand, are quite dry except for occasional thunderstorms, and the mean daily temperature hovers comfortably above 70 degrees near the lake. But the same climate that limits temperature extremes also limits the growth of vegetation. Because of the high elevation (above 6,000 feet), frost restricts the growing season to 70–120 days. The combination of scarce precipitation in summer, the short growing season, and rather poor soil yields slow-growing vegetation that does not replenish itself easily if disturbed or destroyed.

Although vegetation in the basin is mixed because of variations in temperature, precipitation, and soils, coniferous forests dominate. Jeffrey pine and white fir prevail along the west lakeshore. Sugar pine, widespread prior to the advent of logging, remains only in scattered clumps. Incense cedar grows well on the warmer, well-drained slopes, and Sierra juniper, quaking aspen, mountain hemlock, Ponderosa pine, red fir, and lodgepole pine are commonly seen. Subalpine wildflowers and sagebrush coexist in the basin. In addition to forestlands, Tahoe has chaparral, meadows, and marshes.

Many animals and birds originally flourished in this varied habitat, including the many stream tributaries that enter the lake. Grizzly bears, wolverines, peregrine falcons, osprey, goshawks, and many other species of animals and birds were once numerous. The U.S. Forest Service estimates that 275 species of wildlife still inhabit the basin, although several are now listed as rare or endangered. Grizzlies disappeared long ago, and the peregrine falcon and the wolverine, among others, no longer reside in the basin because of the deterioration of their habitat.

Native fisheries largely disappeared, eliminated by overfishing, dams, human interference with spawning grounds, pollution of streams with sawdust, and the competition of exotic fish species. Efforts have been made to reintroduce the native Lahontan cutthroat trout, once the principal species in Lake Tahoe. To encourage a large sports fishery, state fish and game departments have introduced a number of exotic species: rainbow trout, brown trout, Kokanee salmon, lake trout (mackinaw), brook trout, and others.

Barring some unusual natural event like a volcanic eruption or a new glacial epoch, the ecosystem of the basin would change very gradually under natural conditions, remaining relatively stable over millennia. The clarity and purity of Tahoe's water could be maintained for a long time if its ecological cycles remained stable.

The Washoes

According to archaeologist Susan Lindström, Native Americans first set foot on the shores of Lake Tahoe some eight to nine thousand years ago. The Washoes, whose lands centered on the Tahoe Basin and the upper Truckee, Carson, and Walker Rivers, have lived continuously in the region for at least thirteen hundred years. This long tenure may have resulted from their relative isolation and independence from their neighbors, made possible by the diversity and abundance of plants and animals in the region.

Because they lacked domesticated animals, agriculture, and such skills as pottery making and metallurgy, the Washoes depended on hunting, gathering, and fishing. Lindström and other students of the Washoes are learning that the Washoes "may have incorporated horticultural practices (pruning, controlled burning, weeding, seed sowing, etc.) into their foraging/collecting mode, whereby wild plant and animal habitats were consciously managed, maintained and transformed."[2] Undoubtedly, marked climatic changes over centuries, from extended droughts to periods of extensive precipitation, resulted in changing land-use practices.

Needing to reprovision after spending the long winter months encamped in valleys just east of the Sierra, most Washoes made an annual trek to Tahoe as the snows melted and fish began to spawn in the lake's inlets. Scattered groups came together at "Da ow a ga," which means the edge of the lake and which Euro-Americans later mispronounced as Tahoe. Many Washoe families returned to the same campsite each year; their bedrock mortars are still clearly visible today. With an abundance of fish, they could feast, enjoy visiting with their neighbors, and participate in competitive sports, dancing, and courtship.

More than at any other time of the year, the Washoes joined as one people at Tahoe each summer. They regarded the lake as a sacred place, a provider of food, and an important social gathering point. All members of a family would work intensively during the short time when fish swam upstream to spawn. Cutthroat trout and suckers were so plentiful they could be caught easily with two-pronged spears, nets, conical baskets, and even by hand in low water. The portion of the catch not cooked on hot coals and eaten immediately was dried for later use.

With the end of the spawning run and as snow melted at higher elevations, some families left their Tahoe campsites to fish, hunt, and gather seeds, acorns, and other plant foods in the surrounding mountains and foothills to the west. Others returned to lower country along the headwaters of the Carson and Truckee Rivers and elsewhere. The women concentrated on gathering a variety of seeds, berries, leaves, roots, and bulbs. Individual families moved from place to place, harvesting such items as wild onions, potatoes, cattails, sugar pine sap, gooseberries, and sunflower seeds.

As summer wore on and fishing continued to decline, increasing numbers of families returned to river valleys east of the Sierra to hunt for rabbits, deer, pronghorn antelope, and other game and to gather plants yet untouched that season. With the approach of fall, Washoe families congregated again, this time in the piñon forests on the low hills east of Tahoe in what is now western Nevada. Each family collected thousands of pounds of piñon nuts, the main food supply for the winter ahead, and then hauled the nuts to winter camps or villages, each consisting of a few households. They lived in small cone-shaped houses built from interlocking poles and covered with cedar bark or other material. Here they spent long hours making baskets, arrowheads, and other implements as they awaited the spring thaw, when they would once again begin their annual trek to the shores of Lake Tahoe.

Thus the Washoes moved with the seasons, continuing a way of life in the same region for uncounted generations. Only occasionally did intruders or severe food shortage threaten them. If necessary, the Washoes would defend their territory, especially the prized fishing sites at Tahoe and the piñon forests to the east. But normally they remained at peace and resolved internal conflicts by following established customs. While they traded with neighbors in the Great Basin and what became California, even traveling on occasion as far as the Pacific coast for shellfish, the Washoes met almost all their needs on their own lands. Their sense of reverence for and responsibility toward plants and animals contributed significantly to conservation practices that provided a sustained yield over centuries.

The traditional Washoe ways could not be sustained once Euro-Americans began to enter Washoe lands in the 1840s. Rapid change came with the gold seekers who crossed Washoe land in 1848 on the way to California's Mother Lode and later traveled east to Nevada's Comstock Lode. Washoe lands became a thoroughfare, and trading posts and small settlements began to appear at scattered locations, including the shores of Lake Tahoe.

White settlers killed game, claimed Indian fishing grounds, and fenced the land, which they regarded as unowned and unimproved. Their livestock and mine tailings destroyed many of the plants upon which the Indians depended. The mines also became a major market for piñon trees, used for bracing mine shafts and as a source of charcoal in smelting ore. The Washoes lacked the population, political organization, and technology necessary for effective resistance.

Still, the Washoes retained a cultural identity, despite a rapid decline in population by the early twentieth century. Some continued their yearly trek to the shores of Lake Tahoe, where they worked as laborers and domestics, sold fish to resorts and fine-coiled baskets to tourists, and survived as best they could. While their efforts to retain land at Tahoe proved fruitless, the Washoes did acquire small tracts of land near Carson City, Gardnerville, and Reno. In the 1930s they gained federal recognition as a tribe and established a tribal council, beginning a slow recovery. By the end of the century, the tribe numbered approximately fifteen hundred members.

The Washoe dream of having their own land on the shores of Tahoe to which they could return each summer came close to reality in 1997. The United States, through the Forest Service, entered into a thirty-year special-use agreement with the Washoes, providing about 350 acres of Meeks Bay meadow where the Washoes could harvest and care for traditional plant resources, protect traditional properties, and educate their youth and the general public. In addition, the Washoes gained use of acreage at Taylor Creek at south Tahoe, including access to the lakeshore itself, where a long-planned Washoe Cultural Center will be built. Plans include collection of oral histories on land use and management, social organization and beliefs, and other aspects of Washoe life. Tribal chairman Brian Wallace noted, "The future is much brighter for us now—this is an historic period of new hope and boundless possibilities for the future."[3]

Exploration and Early Euro-American Settlement

The discovery of gold at Sutter's Mill in 1848 attracted a flood of travelers to California. Many came via ship; others braved overland travel and the dangerous crossing of the Sierra Nevada on their way to the goldfields. In time, Tahoe gained a share of the traffic from the east, but not until the 1860s, with the reverse migration from California to the Comstock Lode, Virginia City's mining bonanza, did Tahoe become widely known.

No one knows when the first Euro-American set foot in the land of the Washoes. In 1827 the American fur trapper Jedediah Smith made the first crossing of the Sierra, west to east, in the vicinity of Ebbetts Pass, not far south of the Tahoe Basin. Early in 1844, when Lt. John C. Frémont camped near a river that flowed from the mountains to the west of the Great Basin, a Washoe drew a map for him that revealed that the stream originated in a mountain lake (Tahoe) some three or four days' travel away. Frémont led his party south to the Carson River and then, disregarding the Indians' warning of deep snow, west into the mountains. From a high observation point, he made the first known sighting by a Euro-American of Lake Tahoe: "We had a beautiful view of a mountain lake at our feet, about fifteen miles in length, and so entirely surrounded by mountains that we could not discover an outlet."[4]

Later that year, several families (the Stevens-Murphy-Townsend party) forged a new route across the Sierra, following the Truckee River to Donner Lake and then making the first successful wagon crossing of the Sierra in the vicinity of Donner Pass. A small group on horseback, four men and two women, followed the Truckee to its outlet from Lake Tahoe, perhaps the first Euro-Americans to venture onto the shore of the lake. Caught in a mid-November snowstorm, they did not stay long. They skirted the west shore to McKinney Creek and went on their way to Sutter's Fort in the Sacramento Valley.

The discovery of gold in 1848 led to an intensified search for a good route through the northern Sierra, but the Tahoe Basin itself attracted little interest at first. The eastern front of the Sierra, as approached from the Carson Valley, provided a formidable barrier, and anyone who surmounted the Carson Range on the way to Tahoe had to climb a second pass to the west in order to cross the Sierra. Not until the early 1850s did rancher John Calhoun Johnson pioneer a route across Johnson (now Echo) Pass that connected Placerville and Carson Valley. This trail opened the south end of the Tahoe Basin, called Lake Valley.

Martin Smith, a Pennsylvanian, built Tahoe's first log cabin in upper Lake Valley in 1851 in order to provide food and lodging to the few travelers who ventured past. Three years later Asa Hawley, anticipating the construction of a wagon road to Tahoe, settled nearby and opened a trading post. He could claim the distinction of being the only permanent inhabitant at the lake once Smith left for the winter season.

Lake Valley became a stopover point on the road between Carson City and Placerville in the years that followed, but few others settled there. They made little visible impact on the land. In describing the south shore of the lake in summer 1857, a visitor noted: "A dense pine forest extends from the water's edge to the summits of the surrounding mountains, except in some points where a peak of more than ordinary elevation rears its bald head above the waving forest."[5] Two years later a camper rhapsodized about "the most beautiful shore we ever beheld" and noted the complete absence of boats or "improvements" about the lake.[6] Another observer remarked, "All that is now wanted is a few good hotels and boardinghouses, which will no doubt come along in their proper time."[7]

Unlike California's gold rush, the discovery of the Comstock in 1859 had great impact on Tahoe, drawing thousands of people from California to what soon became the state of Nevada. The freighting business, the budding tourist industry, and the lumber industry there all resulted directly from the remarkable growth of Virginia City. Essentially all supplies needed by this instant city had to be transported over the Sierra from California, reversing the earlier east-west traffic. A steady flow of heavily loaded wagons hauled everything from mining machinery, firewood, and food to brass beds, chandeliers, and silk. Prices soared, and fortune hunters poured over Johnson Pass on the way past Lake Tahoe to the bonanza in Nevada.

When William Brewer of the California Geological Survey visited Tahoe in 1863, he estimated that five thousand teamsters had steady employment in the Washoe trade and other commerce to the east of the Sierra. Teams of six to ten horses, mules, or oxen pulled loads of three to eight tons in "huge cumbrous wagons" that clogged the toll road. By the summer of 1864, about a hundred inns and lodging stations lined the route from Placerville, including Yank's Station, Lake House, Lapham's Hotel, and Glenbrook House within the Tahoe Basin.

When the Central Pacific Railroad finished laying tracks across the Sierra north of the Tahoe Basin in the late 1860s, the freight wagon business essentially ended. Many innkeepers along the old wagon route moved to the shoreline of the lake. Here they could provide accommodations in boardinghouses for seasonal workers and vacationing families who were beginning to discover the pleasures of summer in the mountains. It was only a half-day's ride from the hot, dry hills of Nevada's Virginia City to the lake, and Californians, especially San Franciscans, were also beginning to consider Tahoe a summer vacation site.

Easterners, who earlier in the century had discovered such attractions as Niagara Falls, Lake George, the Catskills, and Virginia's Natural Bridge, increasingly turned their attention to the American West. Natural wonders—the hot springs and geysers of Yellowstone, the Big Trees of Calaveras Grove, and especially the cliffs and waterfalls of Yosemite Valley—competed with the cultural attractions of Europe for the tourist trade. And with increasing frequency, tourists to Yosemite included Tahoe on their itineraries.

Steamship travel came of age at Tahoe late in 1872, when two new ships joined the smaller existing steam vessels. The largest steamer, the *Governor Stanford*, carried the mail and followed a regular schedule, stopping at Hot Springs, Tahoe City, Glenbrook, Lake Valley, and Emerald Bay. The ports of call changed somewhat over the years as new resorts appeared, and the boat service continued to attract people to the basin. By the mid-1870s, roads connected major points of interest along the north and south shores. Trails were cut across the rugged slopes of Emerald Bay and around the northeast corner of the lake, completing a circuit of Tahoe.

Growing numbers of eastern visitors joined the members of San Francisco's elite and the wealthy and business interests of the Comstock at the lake's "best" hotels: Glenbrook House (advertised as the Saratoga of the West), the Tallac, and the Grand Central Hotel in

Tahoe City. People of more modest means vacationed in rustic hotels and cottages or camped. By the end of the 1880s, approximately one hundred people a day took the stage from Truckee to Tahoe City. By this time, both the road system and the pattern of settlement were well established.

Mining, Farming, and Fishing

While the focus was shifting from the brief rush of teamsters along the Comstock Road to quieter, family-oriented businesses along the lakeshore, other enterprises encouraged settlement in the Tahoe Basin. In 1863 two prospectors discovered an ore deposit on the east bank of the Truckee River near its junction with Squaw Creek. When William Brewer passed there not long after, he found hundreds of men crowded into Knoxville, a ragged tent community of several saloons, a couple of "hotels," clothing stores, a butcher shop, a bakery, and sundry other enterprises. Despite the great excitement and claims of a second Comstock, Brewer felt the prospects were dim and concluded that he "surely would not invest money" in anything he had seen. He had a similar reaction to Claraville, a mile upstream, and to Centerville and Elizabethtown, sites of supposed silver strikes in the mountains between the north shore of Lake Tahoe and Martis Valley.

Although the shanty towns were quickly abandoned when ore samples proved worthless, several disappointed miners drifted only as far as the north end of the Tahoe Basin, an area visited previously by occasional fur trappers and prospectors. Soon a small community appeared; lots in town reportedly sold for $50 each, a hundred-foot wharf projected into the lake, and in 1864 the Tahoe City Hotel opened. With the completion of the Central Pacific Railroad through Truckee in 1868, the growth of Tahoe City as a resort seemed assured. By 1871 the "city" could boast a hotel, a store, a saloon, a livery stable, and a few scattered homes.

Although mining never became an active enterprise in the basin, markets created by teamsters gave rise to agriculture. At first, small meadowlands and vegetable gardens provisioned the individual toll stations and inns along the Placerville-Carson Road in Lake Valley. As business increased, the land under cultivation and acreage of grasslands used to pasture cattle and dairy cows also expanded.

Soon farms and ranches appeared around the perimeter of the lake wherever wild hay could be harvested and livestock grazed. All over the basin, meadowlands were quickly preempted and put to use, usually in parcels of 160 to 320 acres. Few people paid attention to the exact boundaries of their tracts; many neglected even to acquire legal title. With hay selling by the pound and fresh food at a premium, land changed hands rapidly, and speculation was rampant.

By the early 1870s the *Truckee Republican* reported that fifteen dairies operated at Lake Valley, each with an average of sixty milk cows and forty head of young stock. Farmers shipped butter to Carson City or Virginia City. Each dairy maintained about 500 acres of meadowland from which it harvested wild or timothy hay. With the increasing interest in Tahoe land, the value of the meadowlands rose to as much as $20 per acre, a harbinger of future land-price escalation. By the mid-1870s the dairies of Lake Valley supported two shops at the head of the lake that manufactured containers made of white pine in which to ship the butter to market. In spite of gradual deterioration of the pasturage, livestock grazing remained important well into the twentieth century, and small Tahoe dairies continued to supply local and eastern Sierra markets for several decades.

While cows had comparatively little impact on the land, the same cannot be said of sheep. Beginning in the mid-1860s, sheepherders drove millions of sheep into the meadowlands of the Sierra Nevada, enjoying free pasturage and an absence of governmental controls. They set fires in the fall to clear away brush and deadfall that impeded the movement of their sheep; the fires also stimulated new plant growth for the following season. When the sheep returned in the spring, their sharp hoofs severely damaged meadows. The hungry animals left few grasses in their wake, and overgrazing and fires hindered regeneration of the forest. According to a government inspector, "Evidence respecting the injury done to young tree growth by the present system of grazing is simply overwhelming."[8] By the turn of the century, fewer and fewer flocks were driven to Tahoe due to the deterioration of pasturage.

Fishing provided a small but important industry in the basin, though it flourished only briefly. As soon as the Comstock opened in 1859, Italian, Portuguese, and other commercial fishermen plied the waters of Lake Tahoe near the south shore. Men in small boats hauled in thousands of native trout, which, when not consumed locally, were marketed in Carson Valley and Virginia City. The Washoe Indians reportedly netted large numbers of fish throughout the year in the Upper Truckee River and other inlets, and most of these were sold to local innkeepers.

In ensuing years, Lake Tahoe supported twenty to twenty-five full-time fishermen during the summer season. Many considered the fish supply unlimited. Large shipments of trout were sent to hotel dining rooms as far afield as San Francisco, Chicago, and New York. Sports fishermen also exacted a toll, for there was no legal limit to the number that could be taken by hook and line. One fisherman caught 148 pounds of fish in three hours. An occasional native cutthroat trout weighed more than 20 pounds.

By 1880, the California Fish Commission had placed one hundred thousand whitefish in Tahoe and nearby waters and large numbers of young trout and salmon in the Truckee River. In subsequent years, the commission established two hatcheries at the lake and experimented with the introduction of such new species as eastern brook trout and lake trout (mackinaw). Yet when Chancey Juday investigated fishing conditions at Lake Tahoe in 1904, he found only two species being taken in quantity, lake trout and silver trout. Even so, about eighty boats remained actively engaged in fishing, and commercial fishermen continued to ship fish from the basin.

Not until 1917 did the California legislature ban commercial fishing at Tahoe. By then the damage had been done; the native cutthroat soon verged on extinction. Subsequent large-scale plants of fish in Tahoe proved disappointing: survival rates were low. Perhaps, in a quiet way, the decline of the fish populations signaled the potential impact of growing numbers of people on all native species of the basin.

The Lumber Industry

The lumber industry soon dominated both fishing and agriculture within the Tahoe Basin. Although second-growth timber eventually covered most of the scars left by loggers, little virgin timber survived. Both the vegetation and the eroding slopes on which the timber once stood underwent rapid change.

The earliest mill, established in 1860 at the south end of the lake, supplied building materials for local settlements and trading posts. With the discovery of the Comstock Lode, however, the development of mines and neighboring towns provided an insatiable lumber market. As early as 1861, Augustus Pray and partners built a water-powered sawmill on the east shore at the site now known as Glenbrook. Here they cut as much as ten thousand board feet a day, which they transported by wagon to Carson Valley. The same year, Samuel Clemens (Mark Twain) staked a timber claim nearby, then watched in fascination as it went up in smoke after his unattended campfire jumped out of control. Clemens called Tahoe "the fairest picture the whole earth affords," yet the consequence of his brief sojourn on its shores was the scorching of nearby mountain slopes.

Mining of the Comstock Lode increased the demand for wood. An immense quantity of timber was required for square-set timbering, a mining technique used to shore up the ceilings of underground excavations; quantities of wood were also needed for building materials and fuel for steam pumps in the mines. At the end of the long winter of 1867, Chinese merchants sold the roots of previously cut trees near Virginia City for $60 per cord.

When the scattered piñon and juniper trees near Virginia City and the forest on the east side of the Carson Range fell quickly to loggers and the price of lumber skyrocketed, mining interests looked hungrily at the vast and essentially untouched forests within the Tahoe Basin. The editor of the *Washoe Times* remarked on a visit to the lake: "At present the timber and lumber capabilities of the borders of Lake Tahoe seem illimitable."[9] The only problem was how to transport timber quickly and economically across many miles of rough, steep terrain.

Duane L. Bliss provided a solution. As president and general manager of the Carson and Tahoe Lumber and Fluming Company (CTLFC), he purchased large tracts of timberland on the slopes of the east side of the basin. He also bought the mills at Glenbrook. In time CTLFC held more than 50,000 acres in the basin, including many miles of shoreline, some of which had cost as little as $1.25 per acre. The company purchased additional acreage from the Central Pacific Railroad in the northern and northwestern parts of the basin: alternate sections of land that originally had been granted by the federal government to promote construction of the first transcontinental railroad. Before long, CTLFC had acquired other sections from preemptors who would purchase a half-section of land from the government and then turn it over to the company for a fee. It also purchased acreage from people who took up property under the Timber and Stone Act and other federal and state land laws.

With control of a vast acreage of timberland, the CTLFC next completed construction of a remarkable logging operation under which trees from remote corners of the Tahoe Basin quickly found their way across the rugged mountains to Virginia City. Loggers brought cut trees to the lakeshore by flume, greased skids, or teams of oxen. The logs were gathered in large booms and pulled across the lake by steamer to the Glenbrook mills. The sawed timber was then hauled nearly 9 miles by Bliss's Lake Tahoe Railroad, traveling along narrow gauge track from Glenbrook to a large receiving yard at Spooner Summit, about 1,000 feet higher than the lake. After being dumped into the newly invented V-shaped flume, the wood made the 12-mile journey that included a 3,000-foot drop in elevation to the Carson Valley. Finally, the Virginia and Truckee Railroad, also constructed by Bliss and associates, carried the lumber and cordwood 20 miles to the Comstock market.

Much of the labor for tending flumes and cutting cordwood came from groups of Chinese men, many of whom had worked on construction of the first transcontinental railroad. Prevented from bringing their families from China, these bachelor men lived in camps, especially in the vicinity of Glenbrook, where they planted vegetable gardens and retained as much of their culture as possible.

As CTLFC exhausted the readily available forest near Glenbrook, it extended operations to the south and west sides of the lake. A member of the Wheeler Survey of 1876, one of the federal government's geographical surveys west of the 100th meridian, described a large lumber camp at Sugar Pine Point where trees were cut into 20- to 30-foot sections and hauled to the shore on wagons with solid wooden wheels, pulled by six or eight yoke of oxen. Meeks Bay also became an important collection point for timber to be rafted to Glenbrook.

At Tahoe Valley on the south shore, CTLFC engaged Matthew Gardner and others to supply an immense quantity of lumber. To fulfill his contract, Gardner built a standard-gauge railroad from a pier at the lakeshore (at present-day Camp Richardson) back into the woods along the west side of the valley. An average of seventy-two carloads could be unloaded daily. The rails were constantly shifted to reach uncut forestland until, in the mid-1880s, Gardner's lumber enterprise finally came to an end.

A short distance to the east, George W. Chubbuck built a narrow-gauge railroad from Bijou to tap the timber in the southeast corner of the basin. His Lake Valley Railroad, built in 1886, was soon taken over by CTLFC, which rebuilt it and extended the tracks toward Meyers. At Bijou, the loaded logging cars could be run out on an 1,800-foot pier into the lake, where the logs were dumped into the water.

Although Bliss's mills dominated the Tahoe lumber industry, several other operators cut timber throughout the basin. Walter Scott Hobart organized the Sierra Nevada Wood and Lumber Company and established a mill at Incline at the northeast end of the lake. A narrow-gauge railroad carried logs to the mill from timbered slopes to the northwest and from Sand Harbor, which served as a gathering point for logs from company land at the south end of the basin. From there he shipped timber to the Comstock by an ingenious system. The mill had a double-tracked incline railway. Powered by a stationary forty-horsepower steam engine that operated a bull wheel, the railway hoisted the logs up a steep hill, gaining 1,400 feet in elevation. From the top of the railway the timber was moved via flume and railroad to its destination.

The double-tracked incline railway soon hauled large quantities of lumber. Hobart controlled more than 10,000 acres of timberland and kept 250 loggers busy at the peak of operations, but by the mid-1890s the timber supply was so depleted that the company dismantled its track. The logging operation moved north of the lake to Overton, later called Hobart Mills. Left behind were remnants of the former forest, abandoned mills, decaying flumes, and vertical scars on Incline Mountain still visible from the western side of the lake.

Some time later, the California state forester criticized the logging practices of the Sierra Nevada Wood and Lumber Company—practices not uncommon in the Tahoe Basin. Loggers cut all trees of marketable size, leaving the area nearly denuded. In the process, mostly because of carelessness in felling and skidding trees, they destroyed much of the young growth. Slash, consisting of broken timber, branches, and treetops, remained in a jumbled mass where it fell—a hindrance to the reproduction of new trees and a fire hazard.

At roughly the same time Hobart moved his logging business from the Tahoe Basin, CTLFC closed. Not only had the best of the timberland been cut over, but the primary customer, the Comstock mines, had been in steady decline since the golden years of the 1870s. According to one estimate, more than 70 million board feet of lumber came from Tahoe's mills during the peak year of the boom.

In the late 1890s, when the population of Virginia City declined, abandoned homes were sometimes used for firewood. At the south shore of Tahoe, logging camps, mills, flumes, and railroads lay abandoned among the stumps of cutover land. Nearby acreage, littered with discarded equipment and logging waste, sold for no more than $1.50 an acre. The number of people making a living in the basin dropped sharply, many roads became impassable, and former roadside inns and post offices disappeared. After an investment of an estimated $1 million by Bliss and friends and a short period of great activity, much of the Tahoe Basin again became an area of sparse population and scattered rustic resorts and summer homes. It would be another fifty years before the basin would again experience such momentous changes or destruction.

When E. A. Sterling inspected the basin in 1904, he reported that the forest cover had been significantly changed by lumbering and fires. Only on the inaccessible upper slopes did the original forest remain untouched by lumbermen. In regard to the best timber close to the lake, he remarked: "The forest is much reduced in density; brush and reproduction are competing for possession in the openings; the sugar pine has disappeared almost entirely, and is scantily represented in the reproduction; the finest of the Jeffrey and yellow pine and white fir has been removed, fir production in general [is] replacing the pine; while considerable areas have reverted entirely to brush."[10]

The brush, commonly called chaparral, competed with young seedlings. Fortunately, loggers had left enough defective trees to provide sufficient seed for reproduction. As a result, in the absence of fire, a dense new forest, 10–20 feet high by 1904, had risen. White firs held competitive advantage, producing an abundance of seeds, growing well in the shade, and surviving in relatively poor seedbeds. These trees grew from amid the chaparral and the old slash left by logging operators, providing a forest cover that promised to restore the scenic beauty, if not the quality of timber, that had once graced the slopes of the Tahoe Basin.

But because of the density of the new growth and the abundance of the slash, the new forest was vulnerable to fires as never before. In September 1889, for example, the *Sacramento Record-Union* reported: "Witnesses fresh from the Lake Tahoe region inform us that almost that entire section is a scene of desolation on account of the destruction of fires. . . . At the head of Emerald Bay last week a fire was raging of many miles extent, destroying the finest park of tree growth in all that region."[11] The article noted the potential consequences of the loss of vegetation: floods, soil erosion, reduction in wildlife, destruction of valuable timber, and desolation of the finest scenery.

A fire that started near Meyers in September 1898 swept up the mountains to the east. When Charles H. Shinn, a U.S. forest agent, visited the basin in 1902 he reported many small and smoldering fires, especially on the California side of the basin, often "four to ten in one day's travel."[12] The debris left from logging operations fed the fires, creating sufficient heat to destroy humus and harden clay in the soil. In 1903 a fire southeast of Bijou burned unchecked for more than three weeks.

Sheepherders, who intentionally set many of the fires to encourage the growth of new vegetation, also damaged the forest by bringing their sheep to the mountains early in the season. The animals destroyed more than they ate, sliding on the wet slopes and trampling the young grasses. By autumn no feed remained, and visitors to the basin had to carry hay and barley for their horses.

The damage to young trees as a result of overgrazing was evident. The most overstocked range had almost no new seedlings, whereas ranges spared from overgrazing revealed a mass of young trees, often two or three thousand an acre, that choked out the competing underbrush. The brush was less dense on the more arid east side of the basin and provided a useful ground cover to reduce erosion, although it also hindered second-growth timber.

When forest agent Sterling completed his 1904 investigation, he foresaw little hope for protecting the forest, for he believed that local sentiment opposed state laws to regulate and protect it. He advocated increased federal activity in the basin, at least in the corner already set aside as a forest reserve. By this time, the question of government ownership and regulation of land in the Tahoe Basin had become a critical issue.

Another important legacy of the logging era was a pattern of landownership that affected development around the lake in the twentieth century. On the east shore in particular, Bliss and Hobart had dominated, purchasing their land outright. There, property remained in large blocks; because little could be done with the land after the timber had been removed, there was no reason to divide it for sale. As a consequence, large landholdings were available later for both a state park and a national forest and for such major developments as Incline Village. At the south shore, in contrast, where the right to cut timber had often been leased rather than purchased, landownership tended to be more segmented. Cutover land retained value for grazing, and some tracts on level terrain close to the lake were attractive for building summer cottages. In general, individual landholdings on the California side tended to be smaller than on the east shore, which left the door open for the patchwork of small developments and subdivisions that followed.

The passing of the logging era marked the end of a period in which farmers, sheepherders, miners, fishermen, and loggers attempted to profit from Tahoe's natural resources. Prospectors never found the mineral wealth they sought. Fishermen and sheepherders depleted the resources on which they depended. Loggers quickly decimated the forest and in the process eliminated the employment base it had provided. By the turn of the century, Tahoe no longer offered attractive opportunities for the exploitation of natural resources. Future development, including the urbanization of parts of the basin, rested instead upon the slowly growing tourist trade.

Tourism and Summer Homes

Tourism soon dominated the economic life of Tahoe. Duane Bliss and his family, responding to the collapse of the lumber industry in the basin, shifted their financial interests to the burgeoning summer recreation business. The *Tahoe*, a graceful 169-foot steamship owned by the Blisses, was launched at Glenbrook in 1896. Adorned with the finest brass and mahogany, this elegant ship could carry two hundred passengers at about 20 knots and was aptly called the "queen of the lake." She had Moroccan leather upholstery and fine Belgian carpets; no expense was spared to provide the finest appointments. For nearly forty years, the *Tahoe* made her rounds of the lake, delivering the mail and carrying passengers.

His lake transportation business assured, Bliss linked the Tahoe Basin by rail to the outside world. He dismantled the logging railroads at Glenbrook and the south shore and used the locomotives, cars, rails, and other equipment to enable his Lake Tahoe Railway and Transportation Company to link Truckee to Tahoe City. By 1900 construction crews had laid fifteen miles of track. The new narrow-gauge railroad operated from 15 May to 15 November each year, primarily to serve the tourist trade. The following year the Bliss family completed the final link in its tourist enterprise, the luxurious Tahoe Tavern.

This large, four-story hotel, situated just south of Tahoe City, combined elegance with rusticity. As the Tavern advertised: "Imagine a long rambling building of shingles the color of pine bark, twenty-foot porches, whose supports are the roughhewn native wood, all set in the primeval forest, with the magnificent sweep of Lake Tahoe in front, and you have the picture of this hotel."[13] A San Francisco businessman could leave his family at the Tavern for the summer and commute there on weekends. The Friday night train arrived in time for breakfast at the lake, and the return train on Sunday night took him home in time for work on Monday morning.

Tahoe offered a rare combination of attractions: accessibility, first-class accommodations, and remarkable scenic beauty. A Southern Pacific promotional book noted: "Tahoe is yet of the wilderness, and this is its chief charm. It is at the doors of cities, easy of access and hospitable, provided with the comforts of a luxury-loving age, while preserving the virtues of the simple life and freedom from the scrambling conceits of over refinement."[14]

The Tahoe Tavern continued a tradition of prestigious hotels at Lake Tahoe. The refurbished Tallac Hotel, near present-day Camp Richardson, advertised its own "ballroom, ladies' billiards and pool room, four latest improved bowling alleys, sun parlors, stage and dressing rooms for theatricals, $10,000 worth of French plate mirrors and 500 electric lights."[15]

In spite of the railroad and luxury hotels, major portions of the shoreline remained relatively isolated. Many of the roads used during the logging boom had fallen into disrepair. No road connected the north and south shores, and access to the basin by any means except rail from Truckee to Tahoe City remained uncomfortable and undependable. California clearly needed better transportation and began constructing a state highway system prior to World War I.

The *San Francisco Call* reported in 1913 that a Buick touring car set a speed record from Oakland to Tahoe Tavern, covering close to

250 miles in fourteen hours and forty minutes. In 1919, a Pierce Arrow stage took only four hours to travel from Placerville to Tahoe on "one of the finest mountain roads in all California." Such improved roads helped transform the automobile from a luxury to a convenience, if not a necessity, by the 1920s.

The appearance little by little of several new resorts and roads signaled changes under way within the basin. In 1913, crews finished a road across the cliff above Emerald Bay, and the later completion of an east shore road meant that motorists could circle the lake during the summer months. The older resorts were expensive to maintain and did not offer the accommodations desired by the new wave of tourists arriving by bus and automobile. The Tahoe Tavern continued to cater to its wealthy clientele, but the Tallac Hotel closed its doors in the early 1920s. In its place sprang up such family-oriented areas as Camp Richardson and Meeks Bay Resort, which provided camping and moderately priced accommodations.

As the number of summer resorts gradually increased, so did the number of families looking to the Tahoe Basin for summer home sites. Before the turn of the century, prominent San Franciscans were acquiring private estates near the shores of Tahoe, particularly on the northwest side. Author A. J. Wells predicted that, as at Lake George, Lake Geneva, and Lake Como, "so at Tahoe there will be a summer city, and boulevards about the lake will be builded [sic] and amusement houses will invade the wilderness, and all the gregarious instincts of man will find free play as well as the beauty-loving side of his nature."[16]

Thoughts of the lucrative development of major tracts and subdivisions soon enticed investors to come to Tahoe. In 1906 John T. Read and Brothers, a Reno real estate and mining brokerage, took out a full-page advertisement in the *Daily Nevada State Journal* for their Emerald City Tract, claiming that this tract of eighty-two lots on the north shore of Emerald Bay was the only subdivision of Tahoe property on the market. Seventy-five-foot lakefront lots were offered for $200 to $500 each.

The *San Francisco Call* reported in May 1912 that two leading San Francisco real estate firms had acquired the old Bliss timberland and planned to divide 44,000 acres into large summer villa sites suitable for millionaires and others. In addition, a plan for town sites for people of moderate means led to a prediction that Tahoe would become "a mecca for hundreds of thousands of people every season." An editorial in the *Call* praised the idea, noting that "until now there has been no systematic exploitation of the real estate of the lake shore."[17] Admitting that America had no counterpart to the cultural attractions of Europe, the *Call* nevertheless insisted that America's natural scenery rivaled that of Switzerland, Austria, and Norway. The editorial closed by suggesting that California had a duty to open the Lake Tahoe region to people from less favored regions.

While such grandiose plans failed to materialize, south Tahoe gradually gained popularity. By the early 1930s, Meyers, Al Tahoe, Bijou, and Zephyr Cove were emerging communities, and even Stateline began to show signs of life. Local residents built a small school near the junction of Highways 89 and 50, the first educational facility at south Tahoe since the logging era ended in the 1890s. The school served as many as thirty-five students in summer and six or eight in winter. Classes began in July and continued until mid-December, then closed for three months in the heart of winter and reopened from mid-March until June.

If the local newspaper, the *Tahoe Tattler*, can be believed, the Tahoe Basin experienced a minor building boom prior to American entry into World War II in 1941. The Lake Valley Chamber of Commerce, organized in 1938, provided the south shore with a counterpart to the Chamber of Commerce already operating on the north shore. According to the Lake Tahoe Sierra Association, a booster organization, there were more than forty resorts around the edge of the lake in 1940, nearly all in California. Campgrounds at Camp Richardson and elsewhere proved increasingly popular, and motels multiplied in number.

Not everyone welcomed the signs of growth and change at Tahoe. In a series of articles and editorials in 1938, the *Tattler* complained that uncontrolled growth on the north shore threatened the quality of recreational opportunities at the lake. The newspaper praised those landowners who advocated zoning restrictions at Kings Beach and Carnelian Bay to prevent them from turning into a "desert of brass horns, gaudy umbrellas, [and] rooting tooting pop guzzlers."

The opponents to zoning carried the day, however. There were no legal restrictions on the kinds of structures that could be built, and 25-foot lots appeared in parts of Kings Beach. Each settlement along the shores of the lake promoted its own development with little awareness of how continued growth might affect the lake. The *Tattler*'s editors warned that eventually "something must be done to tie the entire lake community together." No one considered the lake as a whole.

Actually, the building boom of the late 1930s had only a minimal impact on Tahoe's rustic atmosphere. The *Tattler* estimated that fifty new homes had been built throughout the basin in 1939, ranging from a ten-room "palace" to a one-room cabin. Approximately 150 businesses operated on the lakeshores. Tahoe remained a large mountain lake ringed by small, scattered communities. A local dance, the construction of a single home, or the arrival of summer guests to someone's home warranted comment in the local newspaper.

Development of homes and businesses at Tahoe continued to be hampered by inadequacies of the roads both to and within the basin. Tahoe business interests called for road signs and a white line down the center of the narrow roadways. Of more importance, a three-year program to improve Highway 50 over Echo Pass was completed in 1940. The California Highway Commission authorized year-round maintenance for this highway and for Highway 89 from Truckee to Tahoe City, but American entry into World War II delayed implementation for the duration of the hostilities.

Improved highways and the completion of a road around the lake were the death knell for two stalwarts of early Tahoe transportation. The Bliss family railway, which had been taken over by the Southern Pacific Railroad and converted to a standard-gauge track in 1926, could no longer operate competitively despite special winter excursion trains, liberal stopover privileges, and other attractions. The last train from Truckee to Tahoe City ran in 1942; the track was torn up for scrap iron to aid the war effort. Lake steamers, so much a part of

Tahoe tradition, also proved uneconomical, unable to compete with the convenience of automobiles, trucks, and buses. The Bliss family, which had sold the Tahoe Tavern, its railroad, and its steamer in 1925, repurchased the once proud *Tahoe* in 1940 and consigned her to a watery grave in Tahoe's depths rather than have her sold for scrap.

The entry of the United States into World War II and the accompanying gasoline rationing brought activity at Tahoe to a standstill. The lake was deserted except for a few caretakers, occasional tourists, and military personnel. As one resort owner later stated, "We hibernated for five years." Only Highway 40, considered essential for defense purposes, remained open; Highway 50 closed each winter. Even bus service to south Tahoe was terminated. Those who managed to visit Lake Tahoe enjoyed an environment little different from what it had been at the beginning of the century.

Winter Recreation

Skiing, a popular recreational activity within the basin, contributed substantially to its remarkable growth after 1945. Skiing actually began in the Sierra almost as soon as Scandinavian sailors disembarked from ships in San Francisco harbor on their way to dig for gold. John A. Thompson, a Sacramento rancher and a native Norwegian, gained fame as "Snowshoe Thompson," carrying the mail across the Sierra from Placerville to Carson Valley. Using cumbersome 10-foot skis and a single 6-foot pole, Thompson toted a heavy pack in the worst of winter weather. Known for his feats of endurance, he would sleep in shelters along the way or, as the tale has it, dance all night on a rock to keep from freezing in a blizzard. Others introduced downhill skiing. Preferring to compete with one another rather than to duplicate Thompson's feats, downhill skiers ran in short races that became popular in the late 1860s. The Central Pacific advertised a "Grand Excursion to the Snowy Mountains" as soon as its tracks reached the Sierra, and the railroad opened many areas to winter recreation, including Donner Lake and Truckee.

In spite of their early beginnings at Tahoe, winter sports took hold slowly because the first heavy snows each winter essentially closed the basin to the outside world. Tahoe resorts had no regular winter recreational activities. Of course, anyone so inclined could strap on a pair of skis or snowshoes and go into the woods. Ski trails radiated outward from the few resorts willing to provide comfort to winter travelers, but skiing was as much a means of transportation as of recreation. Truckee staged a winter carnival, including ski racing and jumping, in the years before World War I, and both toboggans and skis could be rented at Truckee and Lake Tahoe. In 1928, the Tahoe Tavern sponsored a Christmas fête of ski and bobsled races, hockey contests, exhibition skating, tobogganing, sleigh rides, and other winter sports. By this time, the Southern Pacific Railroad operated "snowball specials" for winter recreationists. Two years later north Tahoe staged its first annual national ski-jumping tournament, with an international field of fifteen contestants and a large number of spectators.

When the U.S. Olympic Committee chose Granlibakken, near Tahoe City, as the site of regional tryouts for the 1932 Winter Olympics, Tahoe began to receive national recognition. Before the end of the decade ski runs appeared at White Hills near Spooner Summit and at Bijou. White Hills offered a T-bar lift, but that commercial advantage was undercut by a lack of snow on the east side of the basin, and the business eventually failed. The small operation at Bijou survived until the ski boom of the 1950s.

Outside the Tahoe Basin, increasing numbers of winter recreationists drove into the mountains to enjoy snow-related activities. The California Ski Association, organized in 1930, staged its first competitive tournament in 1933 under the auspices of the Auburn Ski Club and the Lake Tahoe Ski Club. The association had eighteen member clubs by the end of decade. On Highway 40, lodges built at Norden by the University of California and the Sierra Club near a recently constructed hotel at Soda Springs provided the nucleus for a ski area on Donner Summit. Such nearby ski resorts as Donner Ski Ranch and Sugar Bowl served winter sports enthusiasts. On Highway 50, members of the Placerville Ski Club, founded in 1930, drove as far to ski as the road was open. By 1938 the state kept the road open to Twin Bridges; there a longtime resident jacked up a Model T Ford and operated a rope tow with one of its wheel hubs. At Camp Sacramento, west of Echo Summit, a small ski resort called Edelweiss opened in 1941; it closed during the war, then reopened, featuring the first chair lift near south Tahoe, though it later failed because of insufficient snow.

Roads to both the north and south shores remained open all year following World War II. Several small lifts operated, including at Granlibakken, Meyers, and Echo Summit. Ski resorts had opened nearby at spots like Mount Rose and the Sierra Ski Ranch. By the mid-1950s, some nineteen ski resorts existed in a great loop around and within the Tahoe Basin. Tahoe had become one of the major winter sports areas of the United States.

Four casino owners made a particularly profitable investment when they leased land at the bottom of a wooded mountain that rises to the east of Heavenly Valley Creek on the south shore of the lake. The new Heavenly Valley resort opened in the mid-1950s with two rope tows, a chair lift, and a small hut on top. During the first season ten thousand skiers used the resort, and the firm netted $23,000, largely from the $4 charged for an all-day pass on the chair lift. Twenty years later, the resort was serving ten thousand skiers a day.

Another remarkable development took place just outside the basin in Squaw Valley. The valley had been a hay ranch and dairy farm for decades, ignored by almost everyone. In 1948 Wayne Poulson and Alex Cushing organized the Squaw Valley Development Corporation. Poulson, an avid skier, supplied the land, and Cushing, a New York socialite and lawyer, provided the financial backing. Soon a substantial lodge and chair lift opened to the public. In 1955, to the surprise of nearly everyone, the International Olympic Committee selected Squaw Valley as the site of the 1960 Winter Olympics. An El Dorado County supervisor called it "about the biggest thing that could happen to Lake Tahoe and vicinity." Others noted the millions of dollars of free publicity. The state legislature of California appropriated $1 million to begin a construction program to transform Squaw Valley into a national ski center.

Following the 1960 Winter Olympics, the Tahoe ski industry experienced explosive growth. Winter traffic jams became part of a new way of life. Although the winter population did not equal the crowds of summer, it helped establish a base for year-round business enterprises and a growing permanent population. Together with gambling, winter recreation became the major attraction of the winter tourist trade.

Gambling

Gambling (or "gaming," as the industry likes to call it) was firmly entrenched in Washoe society, well before the pioneers brought their own games of chance to the American West. The Washoes placed bets on any competitive game, wagering anything from a hit on the hand to eagle feathers or even a valuable rabbit-skin blanket. Lumbermen and miners had a reputation for loving to gamble: travelers along the Comstock Road played poker at Yank's Station and other wayside inns. Gambling declined with the end of the lumbering era, but it never completely disappeared.

Nevada legalized gambling in 1869 and banned it in 1910, but from all accounts the changes in legal status made little difference. Clubs in Reno operated as speakeasies, allowing gambling behind closed doors. In 1931 the Nevada legislature legalized gambling once again, at the same time lowering the residency requirement for divorce from six months to six weeks. These measures encouraged Californians to visit Nevada during the hard times of the Great Depression. As historian William Rowley wrote, "Many Renoites tired of causes that sought to protect people from the weaknesses of their own character—penchants for gambling, drinking, disorganized family life, and even prostitution. A sparkling pure city simply was not good business for a mountain and desert town that entertained miners and cowboys and enjoyed a growing divorce industry."[18]

Although gambling in the 1930s was small scale and Las Vegas remained a town of only five thousand people in the southern Nevada desert, gambling eventually became the backbone of Nevada's economy. Harold Smith opened a small casino in Reno in 1936, attracting customers with his "Harold's Club or bust" billboard signs strewn along highways across the West. William Harrah, who had operated a bingo parlor in southern California, moved to Reno in 1937, built a casino business, and soon attracted large crowds. In 1955 Harrah expanded his operation to the Lake Tahoe Basin, where gambling already existed.

Gambling had been an accepted practice at the lake since the early days and continued over the years despite its dubious reputation. Local sheriffs would often arrive too late (so it seemed) to break up illegal gambling activity reported on the California shore. In the mid-1920s, Clyde Beecher built the Nevada Club on the Nevada side of the state line at the south shore, a forerunner of the Tahoe-area casinos. At the state line on the north shore, the Cal-Neva Club emerged in the 1930s as the lake's busiest night spot, attracting celebrities such as Clara Bow and Will Rogers. The *Tahoe Tattler* reported in 1941 that "Lake Tahoe's No. 2 industry is nightlife (No. 1 resorts). To the lake's 20-odd full-fledged nightspots (bars, casinos, dance halls, etc.) flock each week-end an estimated 3000 persons, who spend anywhere from 25 cents for a glass of beer to $50,000 in an expensive game."[19]

This was nothing in comparison to what would follow. After World War II, a number of small casinos appeared at the state line on the south shore. Ownership changed often as businesses failed or were absorbed by neighbors. Eddie Sahati introduced big-name entertainers at his Stateline Country Club. Nearby, the owners of the Gateway Club brought weekend skiers to their casino by bus. The skiers would head for White Hills or Edelweiss in the morning and frequent the casinos at night.

One man proved particularly successful. In 1944, Harvey Gross, a Sacramento butcher, opened Harvey's Wagon Wheel Saloon and Gambling Hall—six slot machines and a few gaming tables in a small wood-frame building. His wife cooked food at their home and served it at their café. Harvey's reportedly provided the only year-round gas pump between Placerville and Carson City. From this beginning came Harvey's Resort Hotel and Casino, which by 1963 served five thousand meals every day and claimed to have more slot machines than any casino in the world.

When William Harrah expanded his business to Tahoe's south shore in 1955, he built a major casino. Operating twenty-four hours a day and providing free bus service from several northern California cities, the casino flourished. The South Shore Room opened in 1959; Red Skelton headlined, and big-name entertainment became the rule. Twenty years after its opening, Harrah's Tahoe had expanded to a 50,000-square-foot casino in an eighteen-story structure with a six-level parking garage, restaurants serving ten thousand meals daily, a convention center, and plans for further growth.

The casinos on the north shore, more isolated from motels and hotels, served by relatively poor roads, and accessible to fewer people, played a secondary role. The Cal-Neva Lodge, purchased by Frank Sinatra in 1960, proved a temporary exception. Stars such as Sammy Davis Jr., Tony Bennett, and Dean Martin played to capacity crowds in the Celebrity Show Room, while Sinatra entertained Marilyn Monroe, Judy Garland, members of the Kennedy family, and other guests. This flamboyant activity proved short-lived, as Sinatra lost his gaming license because of suspected connections with an underworld crime figure.

The impact of gambling on growth within the basin would be difficult to overestimate. Nevada's tourist industry depended on it. The casinos hired an increasing percentage of persons employed around Tahoe. Most lived on the California side, where housing was more available. The growth in population spurred construction of gas stations, motels, laundries, restaurants, liquor stores, and all varieties of service businesses.

Urbanization

Following World War II, business leaders in the basin pondered how to attract tourists and potential residents to an area that had been nearly deserted during the war years. At this time, few if any people understood the potential dangers to the purity of the water or air, and no one foresaw how rapidly the quality of life in the basin would deteriorate. An aerial photograph of the south shore in 1948 revealed only trees. Scattered cabins lay hidden in the woods, but no building broke through the natural canopy of the treetops.

The Rotary Club, the Lake Tahoe Southside Improvement Association, and other booster groups formed to encourage the tourist trade. Most important, business leaders formed a new organization late in 1948 that eventually merged with the old Lake Tahoe Sierra Association to form the Lake Tahoe–Sierra Chamber of Commerce. This group claimed to include nearly all the year-round business interests in the basin; its board of directors represented each of nineteen post office districts at Tahoe. For a brief time the north and south shores seemed to have common interests and to be ready to cooperate.

These new groups sponsored many activities, including an annual summer festival highlighted by hydroplane boat races on the lake. An annual Highway 50 Wagon Train between Tahoe and Placerville, the Auburn-to-Tahoe jeep trip, rodeos, and other seasonal events helped create the image of Tahoe as an "all-year" playground. Tourists could choose from myriad activities, including golf, horseback riding, moonlight boat rides, drive-in cinemas, dancing, and floor shows at the casinos, as well as fishing, camping, and hiking. Skiing increased severalfold during the 1950s alone.

Improved transportation contributed significantly to the rapid expansion, including completion in 1947 of a new all weather road from Echo Summit to Lake Tahoe and along the south shore. The previous year, a Bay City Transport DC-3 made the maiden commercial flight from Oakland to the newly opened Tahoe Sky Harbor Airport.

Spurred by developments such as Heavenly Valley and Harrah's Club and encouraged by employment opportunities in the building trades and the gambling industry, people flocked to Tahoe in the 1950s. Even in midweek, automobiles crowded the limited parking lots next to the casinos. Harrah's buses made three free trips a day, seven days a week, from Stockton and Sacramento to the casino, and the casino planned to double its capacity in 1958. A *Sacramento Bee* writer noted in 1957 that forty real estate dealers stayed busy on the south shore alone, and a thousand new motel and hotel units were added there each year. Thousands of people responded to signs advertising small plots in subdivisions ("$15 down, $15 a month"), while prices of lake frontage climbed to $300 a front foot in preferred locations.

In 1959 the El Dorado Planning Commission approved a master plan for the south end of Lake Tahoe that envisioned a population of 200,000 by 1984, including 50,000 permanent residents, an equal number of summer home residents, and 100,000 tourists. Looking at the entire basin, some members of a bistate commission foresaw a population of 400,000, which would have caused pockets of congestion greater than that of many metropolitan areas in California at that time.

As if in confirmation of these predictions, the Dillingham Corporation launched a huge development project called Tahoe Keys. As described in the *Sacramento Bee*, a massive dredger began a four-year operation to dredge 5 million cubic yards of decomposed granite from marshland to create a one-hundred-fifty-million-dollar residential resort. The machine was to dredge a system of 150-foot-wide lagoons, each 14 feet deep, inland from the mouth of the Upper Truckee River just east of Pope Beach. The developers proposed to provide more than two thousand luxury homesites, as well as a convention site with a multistory hotel, a large marina with winter storage for two thousand boats, and a 30-acre regional shopping center. Although not all of the plans came to fruition, Tahoe Keys became a major development on the shore of the lake. In the process, it destroyed a significant part of the largest marsh habitat in the basin, a natural filtering system for sediments and nutrients carried into the lake.

In the early 1960s, the Lake Tahoe South Shore Chamber of Commerce looked back proudly at what had been achieved on the south shore. The recreation industry continued to spur development. Motels, supermarkets, restaurants, bars, clothing stores, ski rental shops, and many other businesses flourished. Construction, the Chamber of Commerce noted, had "passed the erratic-spurt stage and has now settled into a pattern of solid, dependable development reflecting a stable real estate trend, a predictable population level, and a firming economy in general." Agriculture had nearly disappeared and had been replaced by sheet-metal work, custom furniture manufacturing, automobile sales and service, printing and publishing, advertising art, and public relations. The Chamber of Commerce announced it had launched a carefully planned campaign to attract electronic laboratories and that south Tahoe would become a major convention center.

The north shore also felt the pressures of growth. Lakeshore lots that could be sold for $250 apiece twenty-five years earlier now sold for $400 a front foot. As one newspaper put it, real estate offices were "more numerous than gas stations, taco stands, and Dairy Queen stores combined." At perhaps twelve different locations, subdivisions spread into the hills near the lake as forested areas yielded to the bulldozer and subdivider.

Of greatest significance for the north shore, in 1960 the Crystal Bay Development Company purchased 9,000 acres for $25 million at Incline in the northeastern corner of the basin. This prized land had been purchased in the late 1930s by George Whittell, a wealthy Californian. The *Nevada State Journal* announced that the development company had begun turning the property "into what will eventually become a $300,000,000 chunk of real estate to gladden the heart of the Washoe County assessor."[20] Planner Raymond M. Smith foresaw a 56-acre shopping facility, four or five hotels, a casino area of 20 or 30 acres, a civic or community center, a public park, and space for an apartment and office complex and motels.

By the 1960s the Tahoe Basin was afflicted by runaway growth. The scattered cabins and summer resorts of the early decades of the century had given way to high-rise casino-hotels, year-round tourism, and urban sprawl in certain parts of the basin. But at the same time, private citizens and public officials had been taking steps to keep a large part of the basin undeveloped to protect its scenic and recreational values and the quality of Tahoe's water.

2   Parks, Forests, and Water

Early Environmental Concerns

Most people accepted as a matter of course the changes in the Tahoe Basin that resulted from human habitation and development. A few, however, were disturbed by the damage caused by loggers. When John Muir, the Scotsman who later became America's leading advocate for national parks, passed through the Tahoe Basin in the years between 1873 and 1875, he wrote that of all the glaciated lakes in the Sierra he had seen, "Lake Tahoe is king of them all, not only in size, but in the surpassing beauty of its shores and waters." He also commented that logging "is being pushed so fervently from year to year, almost the entire basin must be stripped ere long of one of its most attractive features."[1]

Most local people expressed more interest in the acquisition of land for profit than in protecting the basin. The *Truckee Republican* complained in 1873 that sections of timberland owned by railroad companies sold at increasing prices, whereas alternate sections retained by the government were practically unavailable except for agriculture and grazing. The difficulty in obtaining timbered land, the *Republican* remarked, hurt the mining interests (and, it might have added, the local lumber companies); the government policy clearly invited fraud and trespass on government property. The newspaper suggested an orderly system of acquisition based on the sale of tracts of land at nominal prices. The Timber and Stone Act of 1878, which permitted the purchase of parcels of 160 acres of timbered and stony land at a low price, met with favorable response.

Yet even local newspapers expressed concern for Tahoe's forests and scenic beauty. An article in the *Truckee Tribune* noted that lumber barons would spend thousands of dollars to visit the Alps but not a dollar to save Tahoe, whose scenery, it said, surpassed that of Europe. In fact, to cut Tahoe's forests seemed a sacrilege:

> If in some old cathedral there was a picture painted and framed by an angel, one such as mortal art never could approach in magnificence, the world would be shocked were some man to take off and sell the marvelous frame. But Tahoe is a picture rarer than ever glittered on cathedral walls; older, fresher and fairer than any works by the old masters, and yet they are cutting away her frame and bearing it away. Have we no State pride to stop the work?[2]

An 1883 resolution in the state assembly declared that it was the state's duty to preserve natural scenery for the health, pleasure, and recreation of both residents and tourists. Further, the resolution decried the denudation of forests along the shores of "Lake Bigler" (Lake Tahoe). As a result, the governor appointed the Lake Bigler Forestry Commission. As the commissioners explained, every aspect of agriculture depended on the water supply, which in turn depended in large part on protection of the state's forestland. The commission's report compared California's forestry problems to those of Switzerland, where destruction of trees had resulted in severe soil erosion, loss of agricultural lands, floods, and filling of river channels.

Although much of the Nevada side of the basin had already been denuded, the California side remained relatively unspoiled. The commissioners urged "preservation of this lovely gem" as well as provision for a "perfect resort" for the state's people and thousands of visitors. To accomplish these goals, they recommended that Congress acquire land owned by the Central Pacific Railroad in the northwest part of the basin and allow the railroad to select lands of equal value outside the basin. California would request ownership or a trusteeship of all federal land on the California side of the basin "for the purpose of forever holding and preserving it as a state park" or state forest.[3] The commissioners felt confident that the federal government would comply because Congress previously had set aside other lands for "public park purposes." With most of the forestland in state hands, it was anticipated that private property owners would no longer have an incentive to invest capital in the railroads, flumes, mills, and wagon roads upon which large-scale logging depended.

The commission thought it advantageous that some of the best lakeshore belonged to wealthy citizens who would value the property more for summer residences and resorts than for the board feet of lumber it might yield. Because the scenic value of privately owned land would be greatly enhanced by preservation of the surrounding area as a great state park or forest, it seemed likely that these property owners would rally behind the commission's plan. A map of the California side of the basin revealed large expanses of land, including considerable shoreline, that had not yet passed into private hands. These lands, the commission proposed, should "come into the possession of the State and remain forever open to the free use of travelers for the purposes of pleasure, rest, recreation, and healthful sport."

The commission's proposal died in the state senate for reasons never fully explained, a golden opportunity lost. The legislature did create a state forestry commission, the first of its kind in the nation. This State Board of Forestry, before being dissolved in 1892, issued reports on destruction caused by unchecked forest fires and on wasteful logging practices. Not until the 1920s did the state once again take a serious interest in the preservation of the California side of the basin, and by then only small segments of the shoreline remained in public hands.

The Lake Tahoe Forest Reserve

In the meantime, the federal government had already taken steps to preserve some of the most scenic regions in the Sierra Nevada. In 1864 Congress granted Yosemite Valley and the Mariposa

Grove of Big Trees to the state of California to be held in perpetuity for the recreational and scenic enjoyment of the public. Congress further established Sequoia, Yosemite, and General Grant National Parks in 1890, well to the south of Lake Tahoe. The next year, a little-noticed rider to a public land act provided the backbone for the future national forestry program by allowing the president to set aside public lands in forest reserves. These reserves were later renamed national forests. Presidents Benjamin Harrison and Grover Cleveland soon proclaimed as public lands the San Gabriel and San Bernardino Reserves in southern California, as well as the vast Sierra Forest Reserve of more than 4 million acres, stretching from Yosemite National Park in the north to a point well south of Sequoia. Although the forestland of the Tahoe Basin remained unprotected, a public campaign was mounted in the late 1890s for its preservation.

Nathan Gilmore, proprietor of a small hotel at Glen Alpine in the proposed scenic reserve, may have initiated the idea, for he offered to give up his own land claims if the president of the United States would incorporate Glen Alpine and environs into a forest reservation. He feared that E. J. Baldwin, proprietor of the Tallac Hotel on the south shore of Lake Tahoe, wanted to gain control of several picturesque small lakes in the southwest corner of the basin. California's two U.S. senators requested that the township in question be made unavailable for private acquisition under federal land laws. This beautiful 36-square-mile block of timbered land included Fallen Leaf Lake and many smaller alpine lakes that stretched into the heavily glaciated Desolation Valley.

Gilmore had substantial allies, including the Sierra Club, a San Francisco–based outing and conservation organization founded by John Muir and others in 1892. Muir had worked actively in support of the Sierra Forest Reserve, and the club worked to protect the Sierra Nevada forests north from Yosemite to beyond Tahoe. In addition, the presidents and many faculty members, alumni, and students from Stanford University and the University of California, Berkeley, sent petitions requesting protection of the township surrounding Glen Alpine. The governor of Nevada, as well as several other state officials and prominent citizens from Carson City, submitted a similar petition. As a result, the General Land Office ordered the land inspected for suitability as a forest reserve.

Central Pacific Railroad agent William H. Mills, although not opposed to the reservation of virgin forests, warned against the possibility of corrupt practices in land exchanges involving private property. Under existing land laws, privately owned land within the boundaries of a forest reservation could be exchanged for an equal acreage of public forestland elsewhere (known as lieu land exchange). Mills feared that private interests would propose forest reservations where their self-interests would be served. He warned that "the whole plan will be transformed into a speculative scheme, and a movement proceeding from esthetic tastes, the love of nature and the instinctive desire to preserve in their native beauty the coniferous forests of our coast will descend to the level of a scramble for illicit personal gain."[4]

In spite of Mills's misgivings, a special federal forest agent, B. F. Allen, proposed a large forest reservation to include all of the California side of the Tahoe Basin from Tahoe City to Camp Richardson. He proposed protecting well over half of the California shoreline and its backcountry, including areas to the west and southwest of the basin, and the headwaters of the American River and lesser streams flowing into the Sacramento Valley.

Local residents and business interests objected, and a number of citizens from El Dorado County, where most of the reserve would be located, sent a petition of protest to the nation's capital. The petitioners had no objection to federal protection of Glen Alpine township, which they viewed as "high, barren, very mountainous and unused except for summer resorts by mountain tourists."[5] But the rest of the land, they believed, would be better left under the care of the county, which would allow private citizens to develop its resources.

In response, Special Agent Allen excluded nearly all the timbered lands of the western slope outside the basin. He also excluded two tiers of townships that bordered the lakeshore, roughly from Meeks Bay to Tahoe City, in which the Central Pacific Railroad owned alternate sections of land. On April 13, 1899, President William McKinley signed the proclamation setting aside 136,335 acres in the southwest part of the basin as the Lake Tahoe Forest Reserve.

The new forest reserve included not only the original Glen Alpine township but also essentially all of what is now the Desolation Wilderness to the east of the Crystal Range—one of the most beautiful and heavily visited wilderness areas in the country. In addition, the reserve incorporated a relatively short but especially beautiful section of Lake Tahoe's shoreline, stretching from Rubicon Bay to Camp Richardson. Lands owned or legally claimed by private individuals were excluded. Creation of the Lake Tahoe Forest Reserve marked the origin of federal activity to protect and manage land within the Tahoe Basin.

Tahoe National Park Proposal

Late in 1899 Senator William M. Stewart of Nevada proposed a Lake Tahoe National Park to include virtually all of the Tahoe Basin as well as extensive forestlands on the western slope. Under the legislation, all surplus waters at Tahoe would be dedicated to irrigation purposes, one of Stewart's central interests. He also advocated development of hydroelectric power for homes and businesses in Reno. Within one year, the U.S. Geological Survey was supposed to survey and prepare plans for a dam, with construction costs to be paid by Nevada. If Lake Tahoe could be turned into a large reservoir, Nevada could reap substantial benefits. The *Reno Evening Gazette*, in addition to praising the protection of the scenery in the area, surmised that the only limits on the potential expansion of farming depended on the height of the proposed Tahoe dam.

Opponents quickly challenged the national park proposal. Although the *San Francisco Examiner* acknowledged that the park bill would benefit the public through protection of roughly 1,300 square miles of timber and would aid irrigation in Nevada, it concluded that the bill rewarded the lumber companies that already had pillaged the Tahoe Basin. Further, the newspaper complained, Stewart's bill included nearly 80,000 acres of "barren, rocky, precipitous land" owned by the Central Pacific Railroad and extending 12 miles west of the Tahoe watershed into an area presumably important to the future economies of El Dorado and Placer Counties.

There had been so much suspicion over the entire lieu land exchange issue that the government was loath to take action. It did not help that Stewart himself had received favors from the Central Pacific and had a close association with lumberman Duane L. Bliss. Even John Muir, an ardent preservationist, feared the "grossest frauds" by the lumber companies against the public interest. As Muir concluded, "Not even for a much desired extension of a reservation should such injustice be for a moment considered."[6] The national park bill languished and died.

National Forest Enlargement

The defeat of the national park proposal had little effect on interest in expansion of the Lake Tahoe Forest Reserve. A forest reserve had two distinct advantages over a national park. First, creation of a park depended on an act of Congress, while a forest reserve could be established simply by presidential proclamation. Second, a park normally excluded commercial development, while a forest reserve allowed uses desired by local business interests such as livestock grazing and logging.

Professor Marsden Manson, a well-known civil engineer and conservationist, described the deplorable condition of Tahoe's forestland:

> Around Lake Tahoe the timbered areas have been entirely swept off, with the exception of a few thousand acres around Tallac, and some at the north end, reserved by the owners for later use. The mountain sides around the Hot Springs [Brockway], and nearly all of the moraines and flats around the south and east side of the lake, have been denuded. These areas, bereft of timber, are now ready to be abandoned to the State, large tracts being for sale at fifty cents per acre. The railroads, which were constructed to carry logs to the

lake, have been torn up, and the region, shorn of its wealth and beauty, has been partly burned over to give a few sprouts to hungry hordes of sheep.[7]

Charles H. Shinn, a government forest inspector, favored expanding the existing 136,335-acre reserve to more than 900,000 acres. He included some forested land in the Truckee Basin to the north, as well as land on the western slope and within the drainage area of the Carson Valley to the east. His proposal gained active support from several groups, especially the California Water and Forest Association. Concerned about the impact of improper use of the Sierra watershed on the farmland below, the association concluded, "The question is a matter of life and death to the Sacramento Valley. There is not enough lumber in all the Sierras to pay for the destruction of the fertility of the valley land."[8]

At its annual convention in 1901, the association endorsed President Theodore Roosevelt's message on forestry, especially the portion stressing the relation between forests and irrigation. Through its quarterly, *Water and Forest,* the association urged the creation of forest reserves from Yosemite north to the Oregon border. Together with the Sierra Club and others, the association alerted the Department of the Interior and President Roosevelt to the magnitude of the problems. When Roosevelt visited Carson City on a western tour in 1903, he remarked that the interests in irrigation "demand the extension of the forest reserve system, so that the source of supply for the great reservoirs and irrigation works may be safe from fire, from overgrazing and from destructive lumbering."[9] In Roosevelt's opinion, the problem of forestry was in many ways the most vital internal problem in the country because lumbering, the nation's fourth-ranked industry, was tied indirectly to agriculture, grazing, and mining.

At the time of Roosevelt's trip, an article in the *Sacramento Evening Bee* argued strongly that a temporary withdrawal of extensive lands in the northern Sierra from settlement, entry, or sale should be made permanent. The article acknowledged the problems of lieu land exchange that earlier had defeated Senator Stewart's national park bill, yet concluded that lieu land exchange for private land-owners was fair because good timber would soon grow again on cut-over land in the Tahoe Basin. In any case, the author noted, "it becomes a question of either holding the forests for the public benefit or allowing them to pass absolutely and irrevocably, in the course of a very few years, into the hands of private owners."[10]

The chief concern in California was economic: how to protect the lumber industry, provide for irrigation, maintain navigation on interior waterways, and promote other vital economic interests related directly to the Sierra watershed. Despite the obvious importance of the forests in California, only three forest reserves existed north of the Tehachapi Mountains: the Sierra (6,400 square miles), the Stanislaus (1,080 square miles), and the Lake Tahoe (213 square miles).

In 1903, Albert F. Potter of the U.S. Bureau of Forestry met with representatives of the California Water and Forest Association, the Sierra Club, the Central Pacific Railroad, the California Gas and Electric Company, the California Chamber of Commerce, state and local government officials, and many other groups. Potter concluded that there was widespread support for expansion of the forest reserves, except by local people. He also reinforced the conclusion that the Tahoe Basin was recovering rapidly from the destruction caused by earlier logging.

In the meantime, Stewart, Bliss, and friends continued their active campaign for an enlarged Lake Tahoe Forest Reserve. Stewart, who continued to champion development of irrigation in Nevada, wrote to President Roosevelt: "Since it has been determined to begin the first irrigation scheme in Nevada on Lake Tahoe, which will make it necessary to raise the Lake about twelve feet, I consider the present an opportune time to consider the advisability of including the Lake and lands within the present Forest Reservation."[11] Stewart compared including Lake Tahoe in a national forest reserve to the earlier setting aside of Yellowstone Lake in Yellowstone National Park.

Early the next year, the Department of the Interior temporarily withdrew from settlement, entry, or sale extensive acreage in the Tahoe Basin. Then, in 1905 Congress passed two bills that affected

Tahoe's future. First, it transferred administration of the forest reserves from the General Land Office in the Department of the Interior to the Bureau of Forestry in the Department of Agriculture. This transfer promised a friendlier policy for resource users. Second, it repealed the controversial lieu land exchange law, under which lumber barons had been able to trade cutover lands for forested public lands elsewhere. This legislation removed the most troublesome obstacle to the creation of forest reserves.

Following the passage of these acts, opposition to new forest reserves declined markedly. Of course, it helped a great deal to have a president who actively supported conservation. During the next three years, Roosevelt doubled the amount of land in forest reserves nationally. On 3 October 1905 he proclaimed the long-awaited major extension of the Lake Tahoe Forest Reserve.

The enlarged boundaries of what became the Tahoe National Forest included much of the California side of the Tahoe Basin except for Lake Valley, today's urbanized zone between Meyers and Stateline, privately owned properties close to the lakeshore, and railroad lands at the north end of the lake. Nearly all the Nevada side of the basin, except the northwest corner, was excluded because the land was already largely in private hands. Nevertheless, by 1905 the federal government had responsibility for substantial lands within the basin.

Later National Park Proposals

Although the U.S. Forest Service administered a growing expanse of forestlands in the Tahoe Basin after 1905, interest in making Tahoe into a national park recurred from time to time. Probably as a result of efforts by the Native Sons of the Golden West and the Sierra Club, in 1912 Congressman Joseph R. Knowland of California introduced a bill to establish a Lake Tahoe National Park. The proposed park included all of the Tahoe Basin except for existing land claims. The bill avoided many of the pitfalls of earlier proposals by omitting large tracts of timber on the western slope, including the most scenic as well as the most sparsely settled mountain region bordering the Tahoe Basin to the south, and choosing borders that would reduce future administrative problems.

Knowland also incorporated several provisions that allowed or left open the possibility of economic benefit from use of the park, such as the right of the government to develop a reclamation project within its borders. In addition, the secretary of the interior could allow leases for summer homes and cottages. Such legislation was not uncommon prior to the establishment of the National Park Service in 1916, for until that time there was no accepted policy for administration of national parks. Knowland's bill attracted little support, however, and when he asked for information about Lake Tahoe, the Department of the Interior declared that it had no publications and referred him to the Southern Pacific Railroad.

Other bills in 1913 and 1918 had no more success, and by the 1920s the idea of a Lake Tahoe National Park seemed dead. Stephen Mather, the first director of the National Park Service and a longtime California resident, had visited Lake Tahoe on several occasions and observed the increasing construction of roads, homes, and businesses, all of which lowered the basin's potential for a park. Besides, Congress was in no mood to authorize new parks; it had already proved difficult to establish Mount McKinley (now called Denali) and Grand Canyon National Parks, which were in relatively pristine condition. Much of the land desired for a park at Tahoe had already been set aside as national forest, and the Park Service did not relish a political struggle with the Forest Service for control of land in the Tahoe Basin. More important, so much of the lakeshore and adjacent lands had passed into private hands that protection of a national park seemed impossible. Finally, in those days, Congress did not appropriate funds to purchase land for parks, a practice that became common only after the Cape Cod National Seashore was established in 1961.

In 1931 Roger Toll of the Park Service visited the "proposed Lake Tahoe National Park area." Toll described the lake as well forested and a "popular summer resort." But because the original wilderness conditions had been "extremely altered" and private ownership was

widespread, and because Toll did not believe Tahoe compared sce-
nically to Crater Lake, he concluded that "this project may be considered closed." Four years later, William Penn Mott Jr. of the National Park Service made the last serious assessment of the basin's
potential for a national park. According to Mott, "private enterprise
and extensive development around the entire border of the lake has
destroyed the possibility of conserving and preserving on a national
scale the natural beauty, character, flora, and fauna of this area."[12]

Mott noted that extensive private lands were distributed among
perhaps two thousand individual owners, and that speculative prices
of $10 and more per acre made the purchase of large tracts impos-
sible. Most of these developments, in his opinion, had been "ruthless
commercial enterprises" that had largely destroyed the charm and
natural character of the land most vital to the proposed park—"the
land immediately adjacent to the lake." No one foresaw that in a relatively few years prices for forestland in the basin would rise a hun-
dredfold and that the price for lake frontage would reach astronomi-
cal figures. It would have made no difference, for in 1935 no money
was available for purchase of parklands. Mott did advise officials of
the U.S. Forest Service and state and local governments to make every effort "to preserve and conserve all that remains of this once gem
of natural beauty."

National Forestland Acquisition

Partly because of the difficulties of administering land that
contained many tracts of privately owned property, the Forest Service launched a program to reacquire some of the lands once owned
by the federal government. Under the General Exchange Act passed
by Congress in 1922, the Forest Service could trade government land
for private property. An alternative method allowed a private land-
owner to receive a cash payment for his or her land from the sale of
national forest timber cut by a third party outside the basin.[13]

Sometimes there were lost opportunities. The Forest Service reportedly failed to get authorization or funding in 1932 to acquire

some 16,000 acres in the area of Crystal Bay and Incline for $350,000. Four years later it again could not obtain authorization to acquire close to 100,000 acres on the east and south sides of the basin for a reported $325,000. In 1937 George Whittell, a multimillionaire from California, purchased much of the land on the Nevada side of the lake for a price reportedly in excess of $1 million. He paid about $12 per front foot for lakeshore property, not an unusual price at the time. Part of this property later became the site of Incline Village. In the 1950s a swampy area of 750 acres near the mouth of the Upper Truckee River became available for $75,000. Seeing little value in the acquisition of a swamp, the Forest Service turned down the opportunity to purchase land soon developed as Tahoe Keys.

Fortunately, in the early 1950s the Forest Service acquired more than 3,500 acres of excellent recreation land on the south shore in exchange for timber valued at close to $1 million to be cut outside the basin. Through the exchange, the government acquired nearly 10,000 feet of lakefront property, including Pope and Baldwin Beaches, as well as extensive shoreline on Fallen Leaf Lake. Most people favored these exchanges except for such interest groups as real estate agents and those who opposed federal landownership.

With the passage of time it became increasingly difficult to exchange lands, as the Forest Service lacked suitable properties for trade. Funds made available by the Land and Water Conservation Fund Act (1964) helped facilitate purchase of thousands of acres on the Nevada side of the basin, primarily from the Whittell estate. The Forest Service also purchased over 10,000 acres in the northwest part of the basin from the Fiberboard Corporation and acquired many other properties, including resorts at Camp Richardson, Meeks Bay, and Zephyr Cove.

The value of the land acquired between 1965 and 1980 approached $50 million, a far cry from the 1930s, when lumber companies offered forestlands at $3 per acre. By 1980 the Forest Service held 65 percent of the land area in the basin, including about 15 percent of the lake's 71 miles of shoreline. Further, over the years, California and Nevada set aside approximately 6 percent of the basin's land in state parks, including several stretches of exceptionally beautiful shoreline.

State Parks

In 1927 California took its first step to set aside land at Tahoe for state park purposes, acquiring a small tract of 13 acres at Tahoe City. The recreation area, originally the site of a fish hatchery, became a heavily used campground strategically located near the crossroads at the north end of the lake. In 1928 the children of Duane L. Bliss offered a gift of scenic land along the west shore of Tahoe, and voters approved matching funds through a state bond. The newly established State Park Commission approved Rubicon Point as the first project on which the state bond money would be spent. After four years of negotiations, the state acquired more than 900 acres of Tahoe's most scenic land, including an extensive stretch of shoreline on Tahoe and Emerald Bay. Prospective campers had to arrive early in the morning and wait to have any chance of finding a vacant campsite in the popular Bliss Park.

Later, in the 1950s, the California Division of Beaches and Parks heard that the property at the head of Emerald Bay, including Fanette Island and the Vikingsholm, was for sale. Considered by many to be the finest example of Scandinavian architecture in the Western Hemisphere, Vikingsholm was a carefully crafted reproduction of a Norse mansion of about A.D. 800. A wealthy widow from Chicago, Mrs. Lora J. Knight, had spared no expense to build the thirty-eight-room house, completed in 1929, where she spent her summers for many years. The property passed to Harvey West, a Placerville lumberman, who generously donated half the value of the 177-acre tract to the state. To this day, Vikingsholm remains a special attraction for visitors willing to walk down a steep road from Highway 89 to the foot of Emerald Bay.

Little of the Tahoe shoreline remained in public ownership by the late 1950s, even with the acquisition of the Emerald Bay property. One outstanding site, the Ehrman Estate at Sugar Pine Point on the west shore of the lake, remained in the hands of a single family for several decades. Because the owners cared so well for their elegant, three-story home and protected the natural condition of the neighboring land, the State Park Commission took a special interest in it. With a growing population of more than eleven million people within a day's drive of Lake Tahoe, no doubt existed about the importance of acquiring new parkland. Aided by a state park and recreation bond act passed in 1964, the state purchased nearly 2,000 acres, including the Ehrman home and 1.5 miles of shoreline, for $8.3 million. The resulting Sugar Pine Point State Park spanned roughly 3.5 miles west of Lake Tahoe along the General Creek watershed leading toward the Desolation Wilderness.

Nevada lagged behind California in creation of state parks at Tahoe, hampered by the extensive privately owned lands on the Nevada side of the basin and a small state budget. In the 1930s the Nevada legislature passed a joint resolution asking Congress to purchase lands at Tahoe for recreational purposes and for construction of an emergency aviation field. In 1941 the legislature asked Congress to set aside, under Forest Service supervision, an area along the eastern shoreline of the lake suitable "for the health and recreation of the people of the State of Nevada." But once again nothing happened.

Because one third of Nevada's population lived within fifty miles of Lake Tahoe, the basin was especially attractive as a recreation area. Recognizing that Tahoe was still in its infancy as a summer and winter playground, a federally sponsored study noted, "The National Park Service, the Forest Service, and the [Nevada] State Park Commission are hopeful that some part of this marvelous area will be set aside and designated as a State park or monument in order that future travelers to the West as well as natives may enjoy the charm of this area."[14]

Not surprisingly, Nevada looked to the federal government for assistance in establishing parks; the federal government owned 88 percent of the state. The State Planning Board and the State Park Commission recommended additional study, in cooperation with federal agencies, of a Lake Tahoe interstate recreational area. They wished to determine what land at Tahoe could be acquired and what administrative policy could be developed with California officials. But the advent of World War II, plus an apparent shortage of funds for federal agencies, discouraged any action.

Much of the cutover timberlands on the Nevada side of the basin had passed into the hands of George Whittell. His property stretched many miles along the shoreline from Crystal Bay in the north to Zephyr Cove in the south, excluding Glenbrook and a few areas in private hands. In 1958 the state of Nevada managed to negotiate an agreement with Whittell for state use of a small beach of fewer than 9 acres. Christened Sand Harbor State Park, it became the first state park on the Nevada shore.

The tenuous condition of the lease, as well as the inadequate size of the beach property, led to renewed efforts to establish a large state park on the Nevada shore. The chairmen of the Nevada and California State Park Commissions discussed the possibility of interstate cooperation. The idea of an interstate park had a precedent in the cooperation of New York and New Jersey in creation of the Palisades Park along the Hudson River. Nevada had the only large expanse of undeveloped shoreline, whereas Californians would use recreational facilities most and help finance the project. The proposal created heated debate in the Nevada legislature, where it died in committee. As a result, the California legislature took no further action on the bill.

In the meantime, the Sierra Club organized a Lake Tahoe Park Committee to publicize the bistate proposal. An article in the *Sierra Club Bulletin* envisaged an interstate park of 35,000 acres with 5,000 campsites. The Nature Conservancy, another environmental organization, offered its services to solicit funds from private foundations and help negotiate purchase of land.

While the Nevada legislature refused to approve the interstate compact, it did approve a Nevada park bill, incorporating the right of eminent domain and an appropriation of $1.5 million for land acquisition and park planning. The park act authorized acquisition of a 13,500-acre tract with 7.5 miles of shoreline between Incline Village and a line approximately parallel to the route of Highway 50 across Spooner Summit. Time was running out; private investors coveted Whittell's property. After further negotiations with Whittell failed, the state of Nevada finally initiated condemnation proceedings against part of his property. A jury verdict favored the state, resulting in the acquisition of roughly 5,000 acres for about $3 million. When other lands were added, Lake Tahoe Nevada State Park encompassed more than 13,000 acres, including some of the most beautiful vistas of the lake.

By the 1970s the combined acreage set aside in state parks and national forests surpassed 70 percent of the land area in the Lake Tahoe Basin. The state parks—D. L. Bliss, Emerald Bay, Sugar Pine Point, Tahoe State Recreation Area, and Lake Tahoe Nevada—offered swimming, camping, hiking, and more. The U.S. Forest Service administered several fine beaches, including Pope, Baldwin, Kiva, and Nevada, as well as extensive areas incorporating most of the mountainous terrain surrounding the lake. Later, the Forest Service, aided by community volunteers, opened the Tallac Historic Site on the south shore. Thousands of people each summer visit its museum, old estates, and gracious grounds. Clearly, parks and forests have come to play a vital role in the life of Tahoe, both in the area of recreation and in efforts to keep portions of the land and lakeshore in a natural and largely undeveloped state.

Dams and Aqueducts

The most precious resource in the American West is neither gold nor oil but water. In the second half of the nineteenth century, farmers downstream from the northern Sierra Nevada in the Central Valley of California and the valleys fed by the Truckee, Carson, and Walker Rivers in Nevada looked for reliable sources of water to irrigate their crops. Miners in both states needed water, particularly for Virginia City's Comstock Lode and for hydraulic mining in California's Mother Lode. Farther afield, San Francisco threatened to outgrow its local water supply and looked to the Sierra for reservoir sites.

One man, Alexis von Schmidt, played a dominant role in early attempts to utilize the water of Lake Tahoe. After he arrived in California with the forty-niners at the age of twenty-eight, Schmidt worked as a civil engineer. After designing an effective local water supply plan for San Francisco and completing other projects, he turned his attention to the Sierra Nevada. In 1863 he proposed that water be piped from Tahoe to Virginia City. When the Board of Aldermen of Virginia City balked at the expense and questioned the feasibility of the project, Schmidt helped establish the Lake Tahoe and San Francisco Water Works Company in 1865 to try to bring Tahoe water to the Bay Area.

Schmidt's proposed mammoth project drew a mixed response. Many found the proposal exciting; others complained about the cost and cautioned that the project could not be completed within the century. The main opposition came from Nevadans who argued that California had no legal right to appropriate the water. The state boundary runs through the lake—the outlet is on the California side, though the water eventually flows into Nevada. The Virginia City *Daily Territorial Enterprise* led a sharp attack on what it called the continuing robbery by a "gang of San Francisco speculators." As its editorial of 2 March 1870 put it: "They may take the gold and silver from our hills, and bind us in vassalage to the caprices of their stock boards, but the pure water that comes to us from Lake Tahoe, that drives our mills and makes glad our waste places, is God's exhaustless gift, and the hand of man cannot deprive us of it."

Actually, sufficient opposition existed within San Francisco itself to kill the proposal, at least temporarily, for citizens anticipated corruption and feared that high taxes would be levied to finance the plan. Elsewhere in California public response was mixed: those who stood to gain were enthusiastic, while others found the idea impractical and suspect. Downstream from Tahoe, citizens of Truckee predicted the ruin of their lumber business if Tahoe water were diverted to San Francisco.

Schmidt argued that the lake had sufficient water for both states and that his company would use Tahoe water for only a few months each year, when runoff from the western slope of the Sierra proved insufficient. By the fall of 1870 a rock-filled timber crib dam controlled the flow of water into the Truckee River. Though Schmidt claimed he constructed and owned the dam, the Donner Boom and Logging Company, essentially a subsidiary of the Central Pacific Railroad, soon had control. The company regulated the water flow to float logs downstream to mills at Truckee.

Others were interested in exploiting the waters of the Tahoe Basin. In the 1870s water was diverted from Echo Lake to the American River and Sacramento and from Marlette Lake to Virginia City. While these two lakes lay well above the elevation of Lake Tahoe, both were located within the Tahoe Basin watershed. In the 1880s the Nevada and Lake Tahoe Water and Manufacturing Company proposed a 4-mile tunnel through the Carson Range to connect Lake Tahoe and Carson Valley, but rivalries between potential water users in Nevada blocked any effective cooperative efforts. In 1890 Francis J. Newlands, later a U.S. senator, proposed a network of reservoirs in the Sierra to serve the future development of Nevada. According to Newlands, Tahoe afforded the "cheapest reservoir space known in the west."

In the 1890s Californians expressed renewed interest in a Tahoe water supply that might now be combined with hydroelectric power generation. An inspection party from San Francisco visited Tahoe in 1900 but concluded that a more accessible water supply could be obtained on the western slope of the Sierra. Continued opposition by Nevadans provided an additional deterrent to any California proposal to tap the supply at Tahoe. San Francisco refused Schmidt's offer to sell for $50,000 the water and property rights still held by his company. Instead, the city launched a campaign to acquire water from Tuolumne River, a plan that led eventually to the infamous Hetch Hetchy Dam in Yosemite National Park.

The defeat of these early proposals to use Lake Tahoe as a mammoth storage reservoir marked the beginning of a heated controversy. Schmidt and others had the engineering skill to carry their plans to completion. What they lacked was adequate financial and political support. Also, the continuing rivalry between Nevada and California discouraged citizens in either state from risking unilateral action; any such action would have been challenged in the courts, if not by vigilantism.

Aerial view of Lake Tahoe in winter. Special Collections, University of Nevada–Reno Library.

Washoe woman basket maker. Washoe basket maker at Fallen Leaf Lake. California Historical Society, Southern Pacific Photo Service, San Francisco, FN-26391.

The steamer Tahoe. *Tourists aboard the steamer* Tahoe *flocked to the rail to view Rubicon Point.* Nevada State Museum, Carson City NV.

Lumber mill at Glenbrook. Lumber mills at Glenbrook in the 1870s and 1880s provided timber for Virginia City and the Comstock Lode. Nevada State Museum, Carson City NV.

The engine Tahoe. *The wood-burning engine* Tahoe
hauled lumber to Spooner Summit. Nevada State Museum,
Carson City NV.

*Tahoe Tavern. The elegant Tahoe Tavern attracted
wealthy tourists to the north shore of Lake Tahoe.*
California Historical Society, Southern Pacific Photo Service,
San Francisco, FN-13684.

Auto travel. Auto travel on the shores of Lake Tahoe proved an adventure in 1916. Courtesy of the California History Room, California State Library, Sacramento, CA.

Nevada Club at Stateline. The Nevada Club at Stateline lay hidden in the forest in the 1930s. Nevada Historical Society, Reno.

View of Tahoe. View from the Nevada shore taken by photographer Truman D. Vencill. Nevada Historical Society, Reno.

Desolation Wilderness. Desolation Wilderness from Angora lookout. James Hildinger, South Lake Tahoe.

Stateline at South Shore. Uncontrolled growth at Stateline (1966) provided strong evidence of the need for an effective regional authority to regulate growth. California Department of Transportation, Sacramento.

Urban sprawl. Urban sprawl at South Tahoe, with Tahoe Keys next to the lake. James Hildinger, South Lake Tahoe.

Tahoe from Emerald Bay Point. The beauty of Lake Tahoe, viewed from Emerald Bay Point. James Hildinger, South Lake Tahoe.

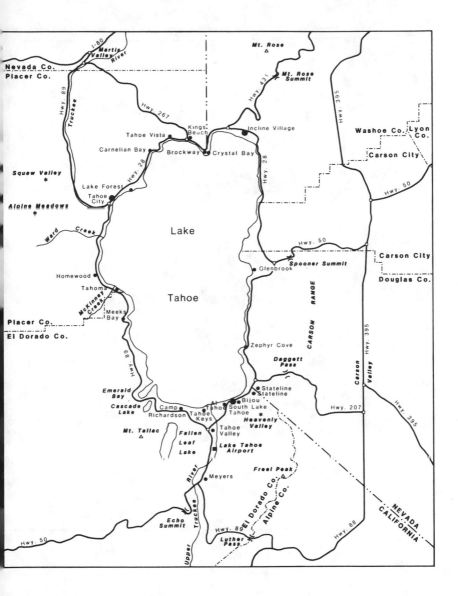

The Lake Tahoe Basin

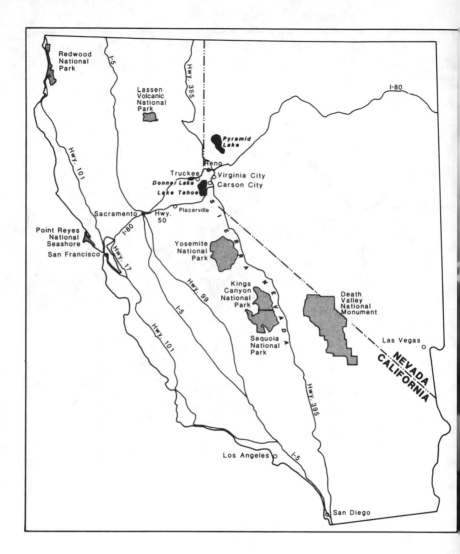

Lake Tahoe in relation to California and western Nevada

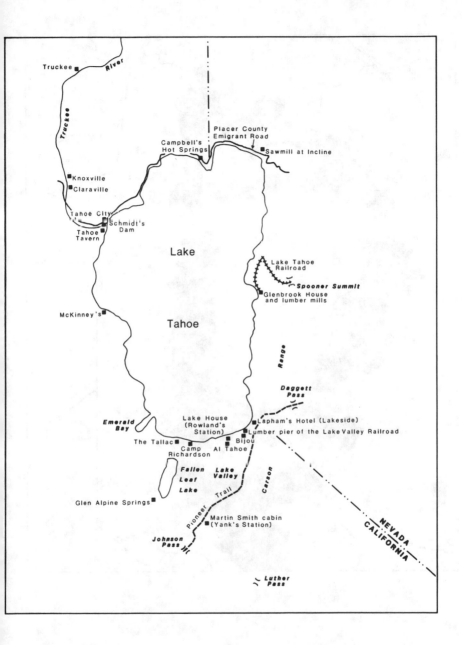

Historical Sites

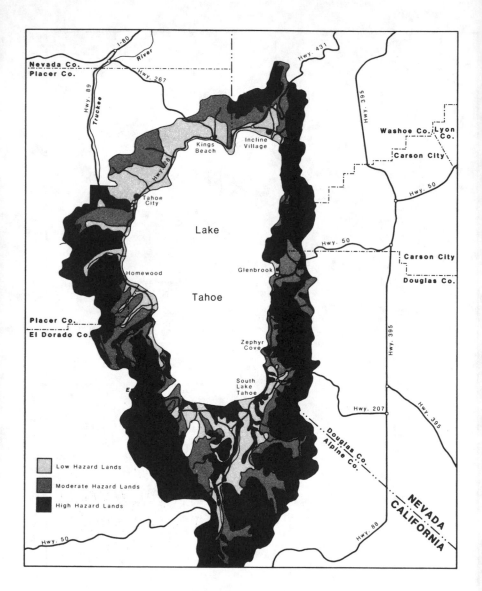

Robert G. Bailey's Land Capability Classification

The Tahoe Water Controversy

In 1902 President Theodore Roosevelt signed the Reclamation Act, a measure through which the federal government provided water for irrigation in the arid and semiarid areas of the American West. Because the author of the act, Senator Newlands, represented Nevada, it is not surprising that the nation's first reclamation project was completed there. In 1905 water began to flow through a 31-mile canal from the Truckee River to the Carson River and on to the Carson Desert, upstream of the Carson Sink, some 60 miles east of Reno. The Newlands Project was intended to open extensive acreage in western Nevada to agriculture, providing the basis for a stable and prosperous economy.

The project depended on an extensive and presumably reliable source of water in the Sierra Nevada, as well as successful application of this water to crops. In 1903 an agent of the Department of the Interior posted a notice of the federal government's right to the water flowing into Tahoe and of the right to control and use at will the water stored in the lake behind the dam. Other parties, however, had a vital interest in Tahoe and objected strongly. Farmers on irrigated lands in Nevada wanted a cheap, dependable, and plentiful supply of water during the season when maximum crop production required it. Power companies along the banks of the Truckee River wanted a steady flow of water for generating hydroelectricity throughout the year. Residents of Reno and Sparks wanted a dependable and clean supply of water for domestic use. Tahoe property owners wanted to maintain the beauty of the lakeshore and to protect their property values and the use of their piers, boathouses, and beaches. The needs of all groups could not be met simultaneously.

The small dam at the outlet of the lake had passed into the hands of the Truckee River General Electric Company, which regulated the water supply to provide a steady source for power generation. Based on this energy source, small entrepreneurs built many processing and manufacturing plants along the banks of the Truckee.

Initial efforts by the government to purchase the dam failed, and federal officials proposed building a separate dam a short distance downstream from the lake. But the power company and wealthy property owners of the area used the courts to block this project, as well as later ploys to bypass the existing dam. In 1909 an eastern syndicate entered into an agreement with the Department of the Interior, providing for government control of the dam in exchange for generous guaranteed water rights. The syndicate also wanted to bore a water tunnel from Tahoe to nearby valleys in Nevada. The *San Francisco Chronicle* echoed the outrage of many when it exclaimed, "Secret Deal with U.S. Puts Tahoe in Syndicate's Clutch." The proposed agreement met defeat, largely because its proponents failed to consult the state of California and Tahoe property owners.

Because of distrust of both the federal government and the eastern syndicate, a group of prominent Tahoe property owners established the Lake Tahoe Protection Association in 1913. This organization, which had existed informally for several years, was the first environmental group created specifically to preserve the lake's beauty. The association hoped to prevent any serious lowering of the lake level. Its objectives also included the protection of fish and game in the basin, prevention of fires, enactment and enforcement of laws preventing pollution of the lake by sewage and garbage, improvement of navigation safety on the lake, construction of better roads and trails, and other measures to keep Tahoe an attractive and enjoyable summer resort area.

Following "friendly" negotiations between the U.S. Bureau of Reclamation and the Truckee River General Electric Company, in 1915 a federal district court awarded the federal government control of a newly constructed concrete dam that still stands at Tahoe City. The ruling assured the power company of a specified flow of water throughout the year. Unfortunately, the 1915 decree ignored other claimants of Tahoe's water. In addition, recurring drought in the following two decades left little water for anyone.

Conflict arose in 1919 and 1920, dry years in which the lake fell to one of its lowest levels in the twentieth century. The Bureau of Reclamation, which had overestimated the amount of water available for the Newlands Project, asked owners of Tahoe shoreline property to sign quitclaims that would release the government from legal penalties for any property damage resulting from use of the lake as a storage reservoir. Alarmed Californians, fearing some nefarious plot by the bureau and perhaps others, met at Tahoe in a mass meeting to discuss the situation and to plan strategy. Representatives appeared from various state and local governmental agencies, local business groups, automobile associations, chambers of commerce, and environmental groups such as the Lake Tahoe Protection Association and the Sierra Club. Obviously, California intended to defend its recreational interests in the Tahoe Basin against the bureau.

Drought conditions recurred, and Nevada farmers had to plead with Californians for a small amount of additional Tahoe water to avert disaster. When the Truckee River east of Reno dwindled to a dry riverbed in the summer of 1930, Nevada farmers sent a crew of men to the lake's outlet in the middle of the night. The men began cutting a diversion ditch with a steam shovel on the property of the Sierra Pacific Power Company (the successor of the Truckee River General Electric Company) to tap the lake below the rim and release water to the farmers. A direct confrontation between the crew and Tahoe residents was narrowly averted when a deputy sheriff used a temporary warrant to stop the steam shovel operator, whom he accused of disturbing the peace.

Tahoe residents rallied in defense of the lake, guarding the rim and the dam after rumors spread that they might be dynamited. On the second night, a group of Tahoe vigilantes stole the magneto from the steam shovel and tried to fill the diversion ditch. Cooler heads prevailed, and a court injunction put a stop to all excavation. The dispute ended temporarily—Nevada was allowed to pump a small amount of water from the lake, and California and Nevada agreed to form an interstate committee to study problems related to Tahoe water.

The controversy led to the Truckee River Agreement (1935) and the Truckee River Final Decree (1944). A number of water users and claimants reached partial agreement on the use of Tahoe's water and the Truckee River. Fortunately, the development of the Boca and other reservoirs in the Truckee River watershed reduced the dependency of Nevada's farmers on Tahoe's water, and the return of normal precipitation temporarily ended the controversy.

After World War II, self-interest and mutual mistrust undermined proposals for compromise between Nevada and California. With rapid population growth in each state and the beginning of a remarkable postwar economic boom at Tahoe, demands on the lake water were greater than ever. In an attempt to find a way out of the deadlock, Congress passed a bill in 1955 establishing the California-Nevada Interstate Compact Commission.

Neither state wished to have the controversial water problems settled in a lengthy court battle. A draft of the proposed compact encouraged development at the lake, essentially set no limit to the water supply available for urban use, and did nothing to control growth. In brief, the commission avoided regional planning, guarded local interests, and protected established water rights.

A formal compact, completed in 1968, was approved by both state legislatures. With a guarantee of more than two thirds of the lake's surplus water, California acquired the water needed for large-scale development of the lucrative recreation industry at Tahoe. In exchange, Nevada gained surplus water for irrigation from the Truckee, Carson, and Walker Rivers. Proponents of the compact in both California and Nevada failed to take seriously objections by the Paiute tribe at Pyramid Lake, whose claim to Tahoe water dated from 1859, or the growing national concern both for Indian rights and for protection of Pyramid Lake. Secretary of the Interior Walter Hickel refused to support the compact, arguing that it neglected the rights of the Paiutes, threatened the ecological health of Pyramid Lake, and adversely limited the influence of the federal government on any future litigation involving the Paiutes' water rights.

Even without congressional approval, the provisions of the compact provided a guide for the distribution of Tahoe's water until the next major negotiation. Late in 1990 Congress enacted legislation intended to resolve the outstanding issues. The Pyramid Lake Tribe would receive a forty-million-dollar settlement fund in exchange for the dismissal of specified litigation. A new operating agreement would be negotiated for managing the Truckee River reservoir system, and an earlier division of Tahoe's water within the basin (23,000 acre-feet to California and 11,000 acre-feet to Nevada annually) would be finalized. The courts ultimately would need to approve the complex settlement before there could be an end to the Tahoe water controversy.

Questions of Water Quality

A new issue arose in the decades following World War II: water quality. In earlier days the purity and clarity of Tahoe's water had been legendary. Visitors marveled at the beauty of the lake, and resort owners advertised the health and vitality of the air and water in the basin. John LeConte, a scientist who visited the lake in 1873, confirmed what everyone could see: the water of Lake Tahoe was very clear and contained no noticeable suspended matter. LeConte could clearly see a white dinner plate more than 100 feet below the surface of the lake.

Even though extensive logging in the two decades after LeConte visited must have created considerable erosion and a temporary decline in water quality, few people bothered to comment on pollution problems at the time. In 1906 Chancey Juday noted while investigating the lake's fisheries that sediment from swollen streams could be traced far into the lake. He commented that Tahoe was "plankton-poor" and that there were few aquatic plants. Apparently logging had little impact on the percolation of water into the soil or on the health of natural wetlands. No one had much reason to be concerned about water quality in the early decades of the twentieth century.

Then, with the construction boom of the midcentury, it became apparent that the people of the Tahoe Basin could no longer avoid considering the immediate and long-term consequences of a growing city along the shores of the lake. Dependence on proliferating septic tanks, with inevitable seepage into the lake and nearby streams, boded ill for the future.

Water pollution at Lake Tahoe posed problems beyond those encountered by most communities. A widespread American waste disposal method, dumping material into a nearby stream to be carried out of sight and out of mind, simply does not work in a basin where the pollutants remain on one's doorstep. The lake has only a limited ability to purify itself. For one thing, the retention and flushing time for Tahoe is roughly 700 years: if the basin were empty, its natural inflow would fill it in about 700 years. Nonbiodegradable pollutants that flow into the lake remain there to the detriment of more than twenty future generations.

Water clarity was also a concern, especially because the beauty of the lake attracted tourists, the backbone of the basin's economy. As nutrients, especially nitrogen and phosphorus, entered the lake in ever-increasing amounts, the danger of eutrophication, a process by which added nutrients increase plant growth and result in deterioration of water quality, increased. Nutrients entered Tahoe from sewage wastes and from runoff caused by disturbance of the mountain slopes, land clearance for buildings, cutting and filling for roads, and many other sources.

In 1946 Nevada's state health engineer warned of the potential of serious contamination of Tahoe's water supply if local communities did not provide adequate sewage systems. Concentration of some fifty to sixty thousand people in the Tahoe Basin in the summer caused the problem. The era of separate sewage disposal by individual property owners had to end. California State Department of Public Health officials expressed a similar concern, and public health officials of both states conferred in the hope of finding a solution. While the two states appointed a Commission on Intergovernmental Relations, which met in 1949, no action of consequence resulted. Key questions remained unresolved. Who would regulate development in the basin and establish a basinwide standard for sewage disposal, and who would finance costly sewage treatment plants?

The rapid increase in people and buildings in the 1950s overwhelmed local efforts to handle the problem of sewage disposal. The utility districts at Tahoe City, north Tahoe, and south Tahoe constructed sewage treatment plants, a step forward, but then disposed of the treated effluent within the basin via infiltration ponds or spray irrigation. An engineering study in 1959, although not implemented at the time, marked an important break with the past in its suggestion of what ultimately became the solution: removal of sewage entirely from the basin.

The report also marked a shift in emphasis from discussion of water quality as essentially a public health problem to discussion of the health of the lake itself. Events of 1959 made this shift timely. The *Tahoe Sierra Tribune* reported that "a heavy infestation of submerged water weeds has become established along the south shore of Lake Tahoe, and much of the recreational value of the beaches could be lost if these weeds continue their spread and growth." This species of aquatic plants, first observed in 1952, had spread rapidly since 1958. They interfered with swimming and boating and drifted onto beaches, leaving them "untidy, foul-smelling and attractive to flies and other insects." Because the plants thrived on a muddy or silty bottom in the shallow water, the low lake level and high summer temperatures may have caused the problem. Erosion from ground disturbed by construction undoubtedly added to it. No wonder some people cast a suspicious eye on a mammoth dredging operation at Tahoe Keys—a 150-million-dollar residential complex under construction in the marsh at the mouth of the Upper Truckee River, a plant-infested area.

In the early 1970s efforts to protect water quality dominated environmental activities within the basin. By this time, however, environmentalists could no longer afford to consider a single issue in isolation from the host of other problems caused by urbanization.

3 Regional Planning and Controlled Growth

Catalyst for Conservation: Emerald Bay

A threat to Emerald Bay proved the initial catalyst for environmental action at Tahoe in the postwar era. Casino and other business interests complained that the existing narrow two-lane west shore road from Tahoe City to Tahoe Valley was slow and dangerous. Worst of all, they complained, winter snows blocked the road for several months every year. Following their success in improving Highway 50, they made their top priority the building of a year-round, west-side freeway with a bridge across the mouth of Emerald Bay.

State Senator Swift Berry of El Dorado County argued that development of Tahoe as a year-round resort and of Squaw Valley for the 1960 Winter Olympics made it imperative to have a good all-year road. Together with the Lake Tahoe Chamber of Commerce, the El Dorado County Board of Supervisors, and others, Berry advocated a low-level route close to the lake. As if to add fuel to their argument, a mammoth earth slide at the head of Emerald Bay in the winter of 1955–56 closed the existing road throughout the following summer. Irate resort owners appealed to the California Highway Commission for action.

Because the proposed road and bridge would cut through both the

D. L. Bliss and Emerald Bay State Parks, the only state parks in the basin at that time, the California State Park Commission had a vital interest in the matter. Newton Drury, chief of the California Division of Beaches and Parks, led a vocal group of environmentalists who opposed what they regarded as a desecration of Tahoe's scenic jewel, Emerald Bay. Homeowners on the west shore, members of environmental organizations, and others joined to defend the integrity of the parks. As an alternative to the low-level bridge route, the State Park Commission recommended a high-level route around the upper end of Emerald Bay, making use of tunnels or snowsheds to cross the slide area. This route would closely follow the existing road, minimizing the need for cuts or fills, as well as eliminating the controversial bridge.

At a time when the California Highway Commission commanded great power and freeway construction proceeded essentially unchecked, construction of a low-level route seemed only a matter of time. Yet a bill introduced in the state legislature to promote the bridge route met defeat in 1958 in the face of rising sympathy for the preservation of Tahoe's state parks. The right-of-way would have eliminated 68 acres from the two parks, almost all of which was shoreline and virgin timberland, cut directly through existing and proposed campgrounds, and destroyed the integrity of both parks.

In 1962 renewed proposals to build a four-lane freeway along the west shore again brought the Emerald Bay bridge issue to the forefront. Late the following year, a group of citizens and landowners organized the Committee to Save the West Shore of Lake Tahoe and lobbied actively to block the proposed multilane freeway, which the committee argued was intended primarily to connect the casinos at the north and south shores. As it turned out, time was on the side of those opposing the west shore freeway. Pressure subsequently mounted in San Francisco and elsewhere in the state against excessive and inappropriate freeway construction that would split neighborhoods and mar the landscape. Although complaints continued about the narrow, winding road around Emerald Bay, no freeway was built.

Postwar Growth and Regional Planning

By the mid-1960s, the trends at Lake Tahoe were ominous. The total population on a busy summer weekend reached an estimated 150,000. As increasing numbers of affluent visitors flocked to the lake, the demand increased for second homes, including condominiums, and for rental property. Land prices escalated rapidly, as did tax assessments, encouraging property owners to subdivide. While gambling remained the largest single attraction for tourists in the basin, the increase in tourist visitation was especially rapid during the winter months, largely because of the improved and expanded ski facilities and the easy north shore access via Interstate 80.

Responses to the growth varied widely. At the south shore, the Chamber of Commerce proudly listed signs of progress, including "six full-service banks; eight large supermarkets; four insurance agencies; a proposed convention and recreation center; two radio stations; branches of Bay Area and Sacramento department and clothing stores, as well as many of our own; a 6500-foot airport runway with 2 major airlines servicing our area; our own savings and loan association; top entertainment and dining facilities . . . which add together to make Tahoe a great place to live."[1]

An article in *Holiday* painted a much less appealing picture when it described Harvey's casino: "Like an incredible tower of tropical fruit, it looms over Highway 50—eleven turquoise stories tall, trimmed with marble and golden aluminum, studded with yellow-railed balconies. A vast wheel-and-longhorn skull device sprawls three stories high across its face; above the hotel roof the emblem appears again, topped by a colossal red neon Harvey's sign."[2] The casino offered employment for 1,600 summer employees, parking for 1,000 cars, and gambling at 1,115 slot machines, 37 blackjack tables, 11 crap tables, 3 roulette wheels, and 2 keno lounges. Across the street, Harrah's Tahoe provided what was believed at that time to be the largest building in the world devoted to gambling.

Nevada planner Raymond M. Smith succinctly summarized the

impact of growth at Tahoe and the need for some kind of control beyond the level of county government:

> A surprisingly large amount of new development is taking place within the Tahoe Basin, apparently, with no relationship to desirable land use patterns, future road locations, future utility or community facility needs; merely, it seems at random. This is, and will result, in faulty community patterns, uneconomic use of the land and other resources and a jumble of attitudes and actions bordering on the chaotic. There is at present no State policy, either in California or Nevada, regarding a regional approach to the problem, although many individual state agencies are concerned and performing valuable work within their fields.[3]

The need for some form of regional planning helped stimulate formation of the League to Save Lake Tahoe in December 1965. The league, an outgrowth of the Tahoe Improvement and Conservation Association, founded in 1957, quickly became and has remained the most active environmental organization dedicated to "preserving the environmental balance, scenic beauty and recreational opportunities of the Lake Tahoe Basin." The membership, composed mainly of Tahoe residents and homeowners and of concerned citizens from elsewhere in northern California and western Nevada, came together to limit expansion of casinos and other developments considered harmful to the natural environment. It sought to curtail proposals for new highways (especially the west shore freeway), promote research related to the decline in water quality, and create an effective regional government for the basin.

Even before creation of the league, Max C. Fleischman, founder of General Foods Corporation and a long-time Tahoe resident, established a foundation in 1951 to encourage efforts to protect the lake. In 1956 Lester Summerfield, president of Fleischman's Foundation, asked Joseph F. McDonald, a retiring Reno newspaper executive, to form a nonprofit organization for Lake Tahoe's protection and "orderly development." After initial signs of cooperation, McDonald encountered vehement opposition within the basin from those who opposed a planning survey of the basin. McDonald concluded that factionalism ran rampant, with south shore interests more concerned about promoting business than about cooperating to protect the lake.

In spite of heated opposition, McDonald helped create the Lake Tahoe Area Council in 1959 to represent all basin interests. The council did not replace any existing agencies or threaten local government. It functioned primarily to encourage research and education related to the lake and to facilitate cooperation in resolving issues. The council, together with the Forest Service and the Tahoe Improvement and Conservation Association, did succeed in persuading the El Dorado County Board of Supervisors to set aside a green belt south of the Pioneer Trail at south Tahoe. McDonald then helped establish regional planning commissions on each side of the basin, and the five counties bordering the lake formed the Tahoe Regional Planning Commission.

The commission, whose powers were only advisory, hired an engineering consulting firm to complete a master plan, *Lake Tahoe 1980 Regional Plan*, issued early in 1964. In the 1960s spirit of growth, the plan allowed for major development within the basin, including divided parkways around the lake. According to a later transportation study, the 1980 plan "was based on the political premise that building a strongly interlinked urban economy was the most desirable future outcome for the region."[4]

The 1980 plan, which shocked some local county planners by its projections of a huge future basin population, did not adequately consider the ecological consequences of continued growth. No way existed to assure that all five counties in the basin (two in California and three in Nevada) would adopt uniform zoning ordinances and act in concert, nor was there a way to control independent agencies like the California Highway Commission, whose actions could have major consequences for Tahoe land use and growth. In fact, the 1980 plan did not legally bind anyone.

While pursuing a basin master plan, the Lake Tahoe Area Council hired Engineering-Science, Incorporated. This firm issued a report entitled *Comprehensive Study on Protection of Water Resources of Lake Tahoe Basin through Controlled Waste Disposal* (1963), one of the most important publications ever issued on Tahoe. Commonly called the McCaughey Report, the study predicted that the amount of nutrients produced by human activity would soon reach levels several times that produced by natural conditions. The established practice of spraying sewage effluent onto land within and near the basin contaminated water supplies and threatened to pollute the lake. By far the best method of effluent disposal, the report noted, was to remove it from the basin entirely. Five agencies then providing sewage services within the basin became nuclei for larger districts to carry out the proposed sewage removal.

The McCaughey Report led to two meetings at Tahoe, first by the President's Water Quality Advisory Board and then by the governors of California and Nevada. The Federal Water Pollution Control Administration then held a conference at Tahoe to help mobilize growing support for water pollution control. A report by this agency noted that the phosphorus level in the lake had reached a critical level and that a substantial increase in nitrogen could destroy the clarity of the lake and greatly accelerate the growth of noxious algae near the shore. Sewage, unfortunately, was not the only cause of the problem; nutrients from land altered by people also contributed heavily. The report concluded: "It is imperative that the man-associated nutrients not be permitted to enter the lake if Lake Tahoe is to remain clear and beautiful."[5]

Not everyone agreed. Two high-ranking officers of the Lahontan Regional Water Quality Control Board, with responsibility for the Tahoe Basin, asserted that there is "no major lake in all the world which has water more crystal clear, pristine pure, unpolluted, and uncontaminated as that which now exists in Lake Tahoe." They continued, "It can be conclusively stated that the clarity of Lake Tahoe has not decreased since the lake was first sampled in 1873—nearly 100 years ago."[6]

Such optimistic claims were challenged by Charles R. Goldman, a limnologist at the University of California, Davis, who argued that the lake's fertility had increased significantly in the 1960s. Goldman noted that aerial photographs showed "spectacular local increases in turbidity due to the inflow of sediments and nutrients from tributaries of disturbed watersheds."[7] He called for a reduction of sediments entering the lake and for export of treated sewage.

Implementation of proposals to protect the water quality of Tahoe took several years. A sewage export system pumped highly treated effluent 27 miles to a reservoir in Alpine County. In 1978 the Tahoe Truckee Sanitation Agency on the north shore opened a sewage treatment facility outside the basin in Martis Valley near Truckee. Sewer districts on the Nevada side of the lake pumped effluent to Carson Valley.

Since sewer districts assumed indebtedness for these projects, they counted on a growing population and increasing tax assessments to help pay the bills. This opened the door to new subdivisions and high density residential and commercial land uses. Some environmentalists wondered if the capital expended on the new sewage systems, especially federal funds, might not have been better spent on buying recreation lands. These lands would have reduced the property available for development and the pressure for an ever-enlarging sewer system.

Local citizens and business interests criticized the Lahontan Regional Water Quality Control Board when it imposed a limit of five hundred new homes to be constructed at south Tahoe in 1977. The board worried about the threat of an overloaded sewer system and violations of state water quality standards. Owners of undeveloped lots fretted that their property would be worthless if they could not get a building permit. In the ongoing conflict over Tahoe's future, the combatants turned, time and again, to the organization that Congress had created to safeguard the lake's future—the Tahoe Regional Planning Agency.

The Tahoe Regional Planning Agency (TRPA)

The water quality problem of the 1960s had sparked tremendous controversy and served as an impetus to create a regional authority for the entire basin. Influenced by the earlier report of the Lake Tahoe Area Council, California assemblyman Edwin Z'Berg called a meeting of the Assembly Committee on Natural Resources, Planning and Public Works, which he chaired. According to his committee's report, there was a "clear need for the creation of some kind of bistate regional authority to govern basin development," an authority with broad powers to develop and enforce a regional master plan. Both California and Nevada legislators agreed to establish a Lake Tahoe Joint Study Committee.

After extensive investigation and discussion, Z'Berg introduced a bill based on the Joint Study Committee's report. The proposed legislation to create a bistate regional agency received broad support from California news media, many legislators, and such organizations as the League to Save Lake Tahoe and the Planning and Conservation League. Advocates recognized that a regional agency could evaluate the effects of future land use on the entire basin and then regulate use to maintain environmental quality. Critics argued that it would curtail the decision-making power of local government and prevent private interests from utilizing the basin's natural resources as they wished.

The city of South Lake Tahoe, incorporated in 1965, led a spirited attack on the Z'Berg bill, arguing that the Tahoe Regional Planning Commission should be the agency to arbitrate problems at Tahoe. But the commission had proven unable to elicit voluntary compliance with its 1980 plan and lacked the power to enforce it. The city council of South Lake Tahoe, for example, adopted a zoning ordinance allowing high-rise development on both sides of Highway 50 near Stateline.

While the California assembly passed Z'Berg's bill in 1967, the senate delayed action. The *San Francisco Examiner* laid part of the blame on Governor Ronald Reagan for his "embarrassing silence" on the Tahoe issue. Apparently Reagan was philosophically opposed to the state's intervention in what he considered a local problem. The *Examiner*, however, insisted that Tahoe was not a local concern and was more than a state problem. The newspaper advocated federal intervention if the bill to establish a regional agency failed.

The state senate finally approved a much amended bill, resulting in the establishment of a much weaker regional agency than originally proposed. In its final form, the legislation established local dominance of a regional supervisory agency that was given neither financial independence nor authority to enforce its decisions. The Nevada legislature adopted a comparable proposal but with even greater power for local governments. One provision provided automatic approval of any proposed development on which the agency failed to take final action in sixty days. For example, if three of the five Nevada board members approved construction of a new casino and all five California members voted against the casino, the stalemate blocked action by the board and thus guaranteed approval of the project. Further, a grandfather clause protected existing casino-hotels as well as Nevada's future right to build casinos on land already zoned for such use. Basically, the Nevada legislature proposed a regional agency with authority to engage in general planning and to review land use but with little enforcement powers.

Z'Berg criticized the provisions introduced by Nevada, which, he stated, "would be tantamount to bowing to the same monied gambling interests and wealthy land speculators" who had worked against his bill in California. He predicted "that failure of local and state government to responsibly manage this great national treasure will lead inevitably and properly to intervention by the federal government."[8]

Eventually a compromise evolved. California accepted the Nevada legislature's relatively weak bistate agency, with a proviso that California could retain the California Tahoe Regional Planning Agency (CTRPA), created in 1967 as a temporary watchdog organization pending approval of the TRPA. Through this provision, California could establish and enforce its own higher standards on the California side and also have an agency to enforce decisions by the bistate group. Placer and El Dorado Counties, fearful that the state organization would usurp local authority, challenged the constitutionality of the CTRPA, a court battle that the counties lost. Nevada had established its own counterpart, the Nevada Tahoe Regional Planning Agency (NTRPA). Finally, on 18 December 1969 President Richard Nixon signed the bill that created the TRPA.

As in most political matters, the legislation received mixed reviews. An early assessment of the act revealed inherent problems:

The conservationists got in the TRPA one of the first regional governments in the United States established for the purpose of environmental control—a bistate agency which sets a precedent for governing the environment. They also got a state agency with comparatively strong powers to regulate the growth in the Lake Tahoe area. On the other hand, the local interests substantially altered the powers originally intended for the state and bistate agencies, gained control of their financing, and acquired firm authority over representation of both agencies.[9]

The priorities of a region financially dependent on tourism and tourist-related businesses and dominated by short-range local interests continued to be in conflict with the goal of protecting the basin from overuse.

Despite these shortcomings, the planning efforts of the 1960s had made headway. Research on Tahoe had advanced significantly, especially through the efforts of the Lake Tahoe Area Council, which acted as a clearinghouse for funds made available by the National Science Foundation and other groups. Publication of its 1963 study provided well-publicized evidence of the decline in water quality of Lake Tahoe. The formation of the Tahoe Regional Planning Commission, however limited in power, at least provided an agency that could consider the basin as a whole. Its 1980 plan, despite shortcomings, was the first general plan for the basin and a guide to later local planning. Finally, the Lake Tahoe Joint Study Committee report made clear the necessity of effective regional government—and the decade ended with the creation of the TRPA.

Regional Planning in Action

Nothing captured the hopes and aroused the suspicions of people concerned with Lake Tahoe in the 1970s as much as the newly created TRPA. The agency inherited an unenviable set of circumstances. The resident population in the basin had doubled in the last decade, and state and federal recreation land use had multiplied eightfold. A guidebook to Lake Tahoe published in 1971 noted that south Tahoe, once an abandoned logging area where land sold for $1.50 per acre, now had numerous motels, as well as "40 gas stations, 52 restaurants, 2 newspapers, 2 radio stations, 7 banks, 8 schools, 16 churches, a hospital, and 69 real estate offices."[10]

Justus K. Smith, first executive director of the TRPA, was given an initial staff of one planner, one draftsman, an engineer, and two secretaries and was told to produce an interim plan in ninety days and a regional plan for the basin in eighteen months. Simultaneously, his staff had to review a continuous flow of proposals for private land development and the construction of roads, utilities, recreation facilities, shoreline development, and outdoor advertising signs.

With a shortage of time and funds, Smith's staff could only paste together a composite of existing maps and plans from local governments. These plans reflected local needs, did not consider the basin as a whole, and did not specify clear limits to population growth. The loosely structured interim plan satisfied no one and provided little guidance to local developers on what to expect or help to environmentalists trying to preserve the region. As one environmentalist commented, the interim plan "can be looked upon either as a nonplan or as a blueprint for catastrophe."[11]

With inadequate resources at his command, Smith turned to the federal government for help, particularly a Forest Service team in the basin with expertise in ecology, hydrology, geology, forestry landscape, and recreational planning. Together, the Forest Service team, the TRPA staff, and consultants developed the Smith plan. This was, in brief, a regional plan to regulate the size and distribution of the future population of the basin, based on levels of use that the land was capable of tolerating without sustaining permanent environmental degradation.

Forest Service geomorphologist Robert G. Bailey devised a land classification system for distinguishing between land safe for development and land that should be left undisturbed. When applied to proposed development, this meant that little or no construction should take place on slopes that were subject to erosion or were in marsh or meadowland. Accordingly, under Bailey's classification,

Tahoe Keys, built at the mouth of the Upper Truckee River, was most hazardous and should never have been built. And Incline Village, with its steep hillsides and construction near streams, was already overbuilt.

Increasingly, in 1970 and 1971 public interest groups that would be affected by the TRPA plan complained that their concerns were receiving little attention. Local people felt alienated and did not trust the influx of outside experts. The agency staff, busy with scientific aspects of its planning duties, failed to build political support in the basin. When the staff finally unveiled its proposed regional plan to an overflow crowd at the Sahara Tahoe Hotel, critics called it illogical, opinionated, utopian, and unjust. In particular they attacked a proposal to restrict resident and visitor population to 134,000 at any given time—the number of people at Tahoe on a busy summer weekend.

Smith soon resigned, forced out by local interests. In time a compromise regional plan emerged. Although the Heikka plan incorporated Bailey's innovative land-capability concept, it more than doubled the Smith plan's proposed population for the basin. Implementation of the Heikka plan depended on adoption of various ordinances ordered in the original bistate compact. As a result, the initial TRPA planning and regulatory efforts proved largely ineffective. So many plans for new developments had received approval during the formation of a regional plan that rapid growth was assured for years to come. As long as economic incentives pushed toward development and no governmental agency stood in the way, urbanization continued.

The Impact of Casinos and Efforts to Control Growth

Gambling sparked development at the start of the 1970s and undoubtedly affected life in the basin more than any other factor. People visited the lake in record-breaking numbers, and summer population of the basin reached an estimated 133,000, including about 26,000 permanent residents. California had 4,500 motel rooms within a half-mile of Stateline; occupancy rates rose with proximity to the casinos.

With gambling revenues rising annually regardless of fluctuations in the national economy, pressure for both new and expanded casinos became a major environmental issue. If the casinos expanded, so would traffic, noise, air and water pollution, and all other aspects of a largely uncontrolled urban development. Even before the first meeting of the TRPA, William Harrah had garnered unanimous support from the Douglas County commissioners for construction of a 31-story, 1,600-room hotel adjacent to his club at Stateline. Following TRPA approval of a scaled-down 18-story building, Harrah remarked, "We believe that what we plan to build is precisely what Tahoe needs. . . . The hotel will stand out no more than the vapor of a jet plane or the silhouette of a ship on the ocean."[12]

Though not yet as crowded, the north shore followed a similar course. Environmentalist William Bronson complained, "Five miles east of the northern state boundary lies the 500-room King's Castle, a $20 million gift to the people of the night from Sir Nathan of Jacobson, as he is called over his paging system, the same gentleman who created Caesar's Palace in Las Vegas. Above lies Incline Village, Boise Cascade's huge, mountain-scarring desecration, beyond which a wall of condominium apartments blocks the view almost all the way to Crystal Bay, where half a dozen, more or less, scruffy casinos crowd the road."[13]

Under the TRPA, construction of casinos proceeded at an unprecedented rate. In a thirteen-month period, the TRPA approved by default under the sixty-day rule three major casino-hotels at the south shore and a major expansion of Harvey's Resort Casino. According to a TRPA staff report, completion of all four projects would result in at least 24,000 new residents, demand for more than 8,000 new housing units, and the need for additional traffic lanes on the California side of Stateline. Because the sewage system was near capacity, much of the needed housing would have to be constructed outside, probably in the Carson Valley. As planner Richard Heikka explained, "What this means is that California is no longer going to be a bedroom for Nevada employees."[14] The new casinos would also demand more of the already scarce water supply and would cause both air and water quality to deteriorate further. A disillusioned state of California brought suit in federal court to block construction of two of the projects, the Hotel Oliver and the Tahoe Palace.

Arguing in support of his proposed hotel, Oliver Kahle stated that he had spent a small fortune in legal fees and planning and now wanted to get his project under way. He reminded California that it had approved the rules for authorizing new construction, and Kahle charged that changing the rules in the middle of the game would be unfair. Besides, he believed his hotel-casino would be beneficial, taking care of upward of half a million people a year. As for housing his two thousand employees, Kahle predicted they would find places to live. In any case, he stated, "It's not my responsibility." He also argued that the multimillion-dollar casinos are the "back-bone that started this lake to what it is today."[15]

The expansion of the casinos led many Californians concerned about the lake's environmental quality to turn to the CTRPA. The California legislature revamped the CTRPA in 1973 to avoid both local control and stalemates in decision making. The legislature also gave CTRPA unusual powers, including approval or denial of all state public works projects within the basin. The "new" agency was directed to develop its own regional plan and to act in defense of the California side of the basin, reviewing public and private projects before they were considered by the TRPA.

The CTRPA encountered a storm of protest in 1974 when it proposed an interim plan restricting construction on the California side to single-family dwellings until the agency had completed its master plan. A crowd of several hundred people roundly booed agency members at a south Tahoe hearing at the local high school. Local businessman Jim Norton expressed community sentiment when he stated, "We don't need people who don't live or pay taxes here to tell us how to deal with our problems." Lloyd Krause, cochairman of a Sierra Club task force for Tahoe, countered that Tahoe belonged to all Californians, not just local residents. Amid catcalls, he stated, "The pursuit of gain by urbanizing Tahoe is not a right. It's a privilege and is revocable at any time."[16] Hearings on building permits attracted large crowds and required the presence of police for security. When building permits were distributed by lot, the slips were drawn by a respected and long-term Catholic priest wearing a blindfold.

A proposed CTRPA master plan provided that no more than 150,000 people should live on the California side of the lake, many fewer than in a TRPA projection. The CTRPA incorporated Robert Bailey's land-capability system into its plan and noted that land-capability and water quality standards could not be exceeded without serious damage to the environment. Local people again protested vehemently, claiming that the plan would block economic progress, injure private property rights, and preempt the power of local government.

When the CTRPA adopted its regional plan, it incorporated a very controversial provision against further approval of subdivision lots until 85 percent of the existing lots within planned subdivisions had been built upon. The city of South Lake Tahoe filed a suit against the CTRPA in federal court challenging the validity of its 85 percent build-out rule. The city also initiated legislation to abolish the agency.

Water Quality and the 208 Plan

While the CTRPA bore the brunt of criticism from local citizens and business interests, other agencies also took controversial actions. In the mid-1970s, the Lahontan Regional Water Quality Control Board, which shared responsibility with the California State Water Quality Control Board for water pollution control on the California side of the Tahoe Basin, banned most new sewer connections. This drastically reduced development. Increasing the load on existing sewage treatment plants risked violating state water quality standards and contracts with the Forest Service and California state parks. In response, the State Department of Real Estate ordered an immediate halt to the sale by developers of 290 unimproved lots to protect unknowing buyers from purchasing property that could possibly never be developed because of lack of available sewer connections.

The construction of new treatment plants and the expansion of existing plants could take several years. Financing them would depend largely on state and federal funding. Roy Hampson, executive officer of the Lahontan board, predicted that the sewage capacity problem would "determine the destiny of Lake Tahoe for the next decade, perhaps longer."[17]

The maintenance of water quality in the basin involved much more than improved sewage treatment plants. In 1972 Congress passed the Federal Water Pollution Control Act, better known as the Clean Water Act, with the objective of restoring and preserving the integrity of the nation's water. Under the act, an agency could seek a grant for 75 percent of the construction costs of publicly owned treatment facilities. Grants required compliance with provisions for the preparation of regional water pollution control plans under section 208 of the act.

In 1974 California and Nevada jointly selected the TRPA as the agency responsible for preparing the 208 plan for the Tahoe Basin. Three years later, the TRPA issued a draft 208 plan that identified several major water pollution problems, including erosion from old logging operations and roads, development in stream environment zones, construction on steep and unstable slopes, and runoff from parking lots and other areas stripped of vegetation.

The TRPA draft proposed a basin user fee to help fund the plan. It also recommended zoning changes to prevent development in stream environment zones and lands with a high erosion hazard. Further, it called for a moratorium on the development of existing subdivisions in stream environment zones until detailed plans to protect these environmentally sensitive areas could be developed. The TRPA governing body, however, gutted the proposal by making enforcement and funding voluntary.

After rejecting the TRPA's 208 plan, the California State Water Resources Control Board (SWRCB) unveiled in 1980 its own 208 plan to prohibit construction on 75 percent of existing undeveloped lots on the California side of the basin. Chairperson Carla Bard explained the necessity for strong action, as sedimentation from construction sites was polluting the lake at an alarming rate. Runoff from developed land and roads had increased one hundred to a thousand times natural levels. "It's as if each day of the year 22 dump trucks back up to the lake and unload," Bard commented.[18]

Under the plan, new subdivisions would be prohibited, lots in high erosion areas or near streams or marshes would be declared unbuildable, and erosion projects costing an estimated $95 million would be carried out over several years. At the request of the TRPA, the SWRCB delayed sending its plan to the Environmental Protection Agency (EPA) for certification. This gave the TRPA an opportunity to adopt a compromise interim plan, to be in effect until adoption of a new regional plan. It applied SWRCB rules to the California side of the basin and left Nevada to make its own evaluation of lots on a case-by-case basis.

Failed Negotiations and Trends at Tahoe

Although several state and federal agencies continued efforts to protect the water quality of Lake Tahoe, the organization most critical to the area's future remained the TRPA. Although the TRPA had been established in a spirit of optimism, hope that it might stem the tide of environmental degradation had faded quickly in the early 1970s. The TRPA allowed frequent variances to its regional plan and ordinances, so the rate of growth of multiple and single-family dwellings did not diminish. It appeared that the TRPA could not or would not stand up to developers.

The League to Save Lake Tahoe responded by withdrawing its endorsement of the agency. The league and the Sierra Club together sued the TRPA, claiming it had violated the bistate compact by approving a faulty regional plan and ordinances that allowed excessive development. The *Los Angeles Times* remarked acidly that the TRPA so far seemed incapable of planning anything but "gambling casinos and shopping centers," and the *San Francisco Chronicle* called the agency an "impotent pygmy." The *Sacramento Bee* added that perhaps the time had finally arrived for the federal government to take over.

Despite these criticisms, the TRPA retained its legal standing. Both the California and Nevada supreme courts declared the agency constitutional, which meant that counties on both sides of the state line would be expected to abide by its decisions. When California failed to block construction of new casinos at south Tahoe, a U.S. District Court judge advised that the state's only remedy lay with the legislative branches of Nevada and California. Thus, creation of an effective bistate agency to control growth depended on revision of the bistate compact that had created the TRPA in the first place, and particularly on changes in the membership and voting provisions that favored local control.

The problem was how to devise a new compact acceptable to both state legislatures, especially when each side distrusted the other. After lengthy negotiations, Nevada Governor Mike O'Callaghan initiated legislation to limit the expansion of gambling, require approval by both states of any development proposal, and eliminate the CTRPA and the NTRPA. California rejected the proposal. It wished to eliminate dominance by local representatives on the TRPA and to continue the CTRPA until the TRPA proved its ability to protect environmental quality at Tahoe.

Charles Warren, newly appointed chair of Jimmy Carter's Council on Environmental Quality, carried on shuttle diplomacy between California and Nevada in the continuing effort to break the deadlock. After months of negotiations, the Warren Task Force optimistically announced an agreement in which state-appointed members would dominate TRPA's governing body, applications for projects lacking majority approval by each state's delegation would be automatically denied, and new casinos would be banned.

Representatives of the south shore casinos who had major influence in the Nevada legislature objected. John Gianottti, Harrah's vice-president for community relations, announced that it would be "very difficult" to obtain legislative support from Nevada unless California made major concessions, particularly regarding the continuation of local control and elimination of the CTRPA. He warned Californians to be under no illusions: "We're never going to leave this lake. Gaming is here, it's going to be here and we're going to stay here."[19] The editors of the *Sacramento Bee* responded by calling the Nevadan pursuit of self-interest "reprehensible" and a path that could turn Tahoe into "just another tacky resort."

With the stalemate, Tahoe continued its growth and resulting decline in environmental quality. The Park Tahoe casino (later renamed Caesar's Palace), approved by the TRPA under the sixty-day rule in 1973, had opened its doors to business in 1978. Luxurious rooms were designed "to make each guest feel like a high roller."[20] Guests found such attractions as marble hot tubs next to their beds, mirrored panels on the ceiling, and televisions in each vanity. Clearly Caesar's did not cater to the outdoor crowd. The Stateline area reportedly enjoyed more than a 60 percent increase in gambling tables and slot machines in a four-year period, aided by expansion within existing casinos. Proposals for massive parking structures by the big four (Harrah's, Harvey's, Sahara Tahoe, and Park Tahoe) threatened to more than double parking space to house 14,600 cars. Harrah's proposed seven-level garage alone would surpass the existing parking capacity at the San Francisco International Airport. The TRPA, once again, proved unable or unwilling to say no.

While the TRPA limped along at the end of the 1970s, environmentalists continued to look to the federal government for help. The EPA had issued a major report, the *Lake Tahoe Study*, which stressed that the TRPA's failures originated in the flawed compact that had created it. The study recommended that Congress declare a federal policy for the preservation of the ecological integrity of Lake Tahoe. It recommended the development and establishment of "environmental thresholds" to keep growth within the boundaries of federal and state standards. The report argued that treating environmental problems in isolation when in fact they were interrelated no longer seemed reasonable. Instead of measuring air and water quality against some fixed standard, for example, the rate and direction of the changes could be studied. Then corrective action could be taken before a certain threshold of environmental quality had been exceeded.

In 1978 the Western Federal Regional Council, composed of representatives from federal agencies in the west, issued the *Federal Policy for the Lake Tahoe Basin*. It declared the basin "a unique scenic and recreation resource of regional and national significance" and called for an expanded federal role to encourage others to cooperate in maintaining environmental quality standards and to protect the uniqueness of Tahoe. The need for such cooperation was made abundantly clear in the council's *Lake Tahoe Environmental Assessment*. Based on the years 1970–78, the study revealed ominous trends. The permanent population of the basin neared 60,000, and estimates of peak summer population varied from 120,000 to 220,000. With more than seven million people within a four-hour drive of Tahoe, a reduction in traffic seemed unlikely. It had, in fact, increased 80 percent during the study period.

Already the basin was violating national ambient air quality standards for carbon dioxide and ozone, and it barely met federal standards for particulates. Water quality also continued to decline rapidly in violation of federal and state nondegradation policies. Algal concentrations had increased 150 percent between 1969 and 1975, and water clarity continued to decline.

Trends in land use were also alarming. The area of urban development had increased by 78 percent since 1970. In fact, since settlement first began in the basin, approximately 75 percent of all marshes, 50 percent of meadowlands, and 15 percent of forests had been converted to urban use or had been significantly damaged by human activity. The removal of vegetation disturbed the forest ecosystem and increased erosion. Not surprisingly, nitrogen runoff, a major threat to the lake's purity, was highest from the most developed land.

Clearly, the gambling industry contributed significantly to the environmental problems, including the sharp decline in air and water quality. An estimated 61 percent of visitors to the basin gambled, and the gambling industry continued to dominate the economy of the area. As the Western Federal Regional Council's report noted, "Gaming accounts for about 78 percent of the jobs, 41 percent of the houses, 31 percent of the tax revenues, and 43 percent of the sewage flows."[21]

What most disturbed the council were the *trends* at Lake Tahoe. The accumulation of seemingly minor decisions and activities had caused environmental problems of major magnitude. Yet there seemed no end in sight to the process by which separate decisions, often by well-meaning people, led inevitably to the degradation of the land and the lake.

The Federal Response

Concern for deforestation and Tahoe's water supply was what first aroused federal interest in the basin. The U.S. Forest Service alone administered nearly half the land in the basin by the 1960s, although it owned little of the shoreline that needed protection most. Many other federal agencies also had active interests in the basin, but the national government wanted state and local governments to settle most of the problems.

The record of the Forest Service in managing basin lands to protect their scenic qualities and curb excessive development had been mixed. For example, encouragement of such ski resorts as Heavenly Valley in the national forest greatly facilitated growth of the basin's all-year economy and increased urbanization. The Forest Service operated under the directive of multiple use—a concept vaguely defined as management of resources so they are utilized in the combination that best meets the present and future needs of the American people. Such a definition left great latitude for interpretation but tended to encourage maximization of use. Following Secretary of the Interior Stewart Udall's visit to the basin in the early 1960s, the Lake Tahoe Area Council announced that Tahoe would receive high priority among several areas to be studied as possible sites for national lakeshore designation. Cape Cod National Seashore in Massachusetts provided an example of an area where problems similar to those at Tahoe were being overcome. It was hoped that existing residential and commercial land use could be integrated with a scenic public recreation area.

In 1969 Nevada senator Alan Bible initiated consideration of a national lakeshore or recreation area at Lake Tahoe. Under the proposed legislation, the secretary of the interior, in close cooperation with the TRPA and other government agencies, would determine which lands should be converted to public ownership and how they should be managed. Key questions included how to balance federal and state responsibility and whether the best designation would be a national lakeshore under the National Park Service or a national recreation area under the Forest Service.

A draft report by the Bureau of Outdoor Recreation (BOR) in 1971 recommended that a Tahoe national lakeshore be established to encompass the entire basin and that $70 million be spent there, primarily to purchase land and easements. In addition, the report recommended a number of significant changes: no more construction in extensive "landscape conservation" zones, pedestrian access every half-mile of lakeshore, provision for bus transportation, no expansion of the existing highway system, height standards on all new buildings in urban zones, no construction that would block a view of the lake from the highway around its borders, and burial of all new utility and transmission lines.

This draft report disappeared in the bureaucratic maze of the nation's capital to be replaced by a final BOR report that recommended against a national lakeshore. Concluding that a lakeshore "would be counter to the desires and interests of local and regional governments," the final report stated that the TRPA as presently constituted could effectively control Tahoe's environmental problems. The *Los Angeles Times* and the *Sacramento Bee* criticized the timidity of the federal government. Such failure to act, the *Bee* noted, would never have saved Yosemite, Grand Canyon, or other scenic areas of national significance.

Despite the ineffectiveness of the final BOR report, the federal role at Tahoe became more overt. Jack Deinema of the Forest Service told the TRPA governing board that Tahoe was an area of "national significance" where the public interest should be fully protected. The Forest Service deferred development of national forestland; the Army Corps of Engineers placed a moratorium on issuance of permits for piers and other structures along the shoreline; and the Department of Housing and Urban Development imposed a moratorium on Federal Housing Administration mortgage-insurance programs in the basin pending effective control of environmental problems by the TRPA.

Thus, although Congress never articulated a specific policy for Tahoe, several agencies took action on an ad hoc basis.

In addition, in 1972 California senator John Tunney presided over a hearing of the Senate Air and Water Pollution Subcommittee at the Cal-Neva Hotel and called attention to the severity of Tahoe's problems. He favored granting the EPA more power to control excessive development. It appeared that federal agencies would be playing an increasingly important role in protecting Tahoe.

In 1977 California's secretary of resources, Huey Johnson, argued that Tahoe was no less a national treasure than the Everglades of Florida or the Point Reyes National Seashore in California. He stated that "establishment of a national recreation area managed by the U.S. Forest Service is the only course which promises a solution."[22] A national recreation area (NRA), in his opinion, would preserve the lake and surrounding land, provide a means to purchase private lands that were prohibited from being developed, improve land management, and allow continued public use of the basin.

The national recreation area concept already had a successful track record, including California's Golden Gate. Under Johnson's proposal, private development, including casinos, would be limited, and a plan would be developed to "restore and preserve the magnificence of Lake Tahoe." The Johnson plan received favorable comment in most parts of California, met with skepticism and caution in Nevada, and aroused hostility from local government officials and business interests in the basin.

Failure to act on a national lakeshore or recreation area did not mark a withdrawal of federal activity from the Tahoe basin. On the contrary, the Forest Service took steps to improve its administrative effectiveness. In 1973 it established the Lake Tahoe Basin Management Unit (LTBMU) to administer the three national forests within the basin (Tahoe, Eldorado, and Toiyabe) as a single unit. This arrangement allowed for coordination of policies on the three forests and more efficient decision making. Starting with a budget of $600,000 and a staff of eighteen full-time employees, the LTBMU administered more than half the land in the basin, an area increased yearly through an active land acquisition program.

When the Forest Service issued a *Land Management Plan* (1978) for national forests in the basin, it emphasized protecting the water quality of Lake Tahoe and preserving the diversity and health of biotic communities and cultural resources. For example, the timber management goal called for maintenance of a "healthy, diverse timber stand of high scenic quality for watershed protection, recreation use and enjoyment, and wildlife habitat, rather than [for] its value for wood fiber production."[23] The plan also allowed for the expansion of recreational facilities on public lands to better meet the needs of visitors. Among many specific recommendations, the report called for the expansion of public ownership in the basin to approximately 85 percent of the land and for use of the land-capability system as a guide in the development and use of federal lands. The Forest Service had no control over the use of private lands, so it recommended continued cooperation with state, regional, and local governments to resolve environmental problems there.

Only one part of the basin remained largely unaffected by the ongoing political battles over development and control of growth: the Desolation Wilderness. In 1931 the Forest Service classified more than 41,383 acres as a roadless primitive area, designating it the Desolation Valley Primitive Area. In 1969, when the tract was enlarged to more than 63,000 acres and made part of the National Wilderness Preservation System, it became the Desolation Wilderness. The main crest of the Sierra Nevada bisects the wilderness area; only its eastern part rests within the Tahoe Basin. Just to the west of the crest lies a deep glacial trench that extends from Rockbound Valley in the north to Desolation Valley in the south. This rugged mountain area, sprinkled with alpine lakes, became so popular that visitation doubled within three years in the late 1960s, threatening to exceed the carrying capacity of the land. By 1971 the Forest Service required permits for anyone entering the wilderness. Proximity to large population centers in California as well as to Lake Tahoe made the Desolation Wilderness the most heavily used wilderness area for its size in the country—and unusually difficult to protect from overuse.

4 Seeking New Ground

Compromise and New Life for the TRPA

At the start of the 1980s, proponents of a new policy at Tahoe had two main alternatives: continue to pursue increased federal involvement in the basin, in spite of opposition from Nevada's congressional delegation and many local people, or continue negotiations on revision of the bistate compact. They pursued both avenues.

To foster solutions to environmental problems (solutions dependent on the cooperation of numerous government agencies at all levels), President Jimmy Carter created the Lake Tahoe Federal Coordinating Council. The Reagan landslide in the fall of 1980, however, foreshadowed a sharp shift in federal environmental policy. Favoring state and local control, Reagan quickly rescinded the order creating the council.

That same year, California congressman Vic Fazio introduced legislation to create a national scenic area at Lake Tahoe. Under his proposal, the Forest Service would manage the basin as a scenic and recreation area. In the meantime, it would administer a moratorium on all major construction. The service would have the power to stop harmful development and to purchase undeveloped private property for the national scenic area.

When this proposal met defeat, the Forest Service helped resurrect negotiations about the bistate compact. Working quietly behind the scenes, service officials arranged for meetings between California state senator John Garamendi and assemblyman Victor Calvo and

Nevada state senator "Spike" Wilson and assemblyman Joe Dini. Drafts and redrafts of the proposal crossed the border between the two states until the final language was hammered out. After approval by the legislatures of both states, Congress passed the measure, which became law in December 1980.

The legislation, based largely on the recommendations of the Warren Task Force, ended the dominance of local interests over the TRPA's governing body. It changed voting procedures to eliminate the sixty-day rule that had allowed for automatic approval of major projects on which the two states disagreed. It also banned new casinos. In addition, it created a Tahoe Transportation District to own and operate a public transportation system and mandated a regional transportation plan that would reduce automobile traffic and air pollution. The revised compact required the establishment of environmental thresholds and carrying capacities and the development of a new plan and ordinances to achieve these standards. Thus the 1980s started with new hope for Tahoe's future.

Such a breakthrough can be attributed to several factors. Undoubtedly the dire predictions presented in the *Lake Tahoe Environmental Assessment* (1979) had an impact on everyone who cared for the lake. Many people recognized that the original compact had proved ineffective. Nevada's political and business leaders made a major concession in withdrawing support for new casinos. Some recognized that Tahoe's environmental quality could not tolerate such development, while others feared that the national scenic area proposal might gain momentum if they did not reach a compromise. Many casino owners understood that the beauty of the lake was key to their future business success, especially since customers had growing opportunities to pursue gaming elsewhere in more than half the country. For their part, local California interests preferred a revised TRPA to continuation of controls imposed by the CTRPA. Local property owners took heart that federal and state funding might allow for purchase of lots that had been designated unbuildable. In brief, growing knowledge of Tahoe's plight, a lessening of hostilities among interested parties, and skillful negotiations opened the door to compromise. The compact gave the TRPA new life; at the same time, a provision stipulated that California's strong CTRPA would be phased out upon adoption of ordinances to implement a new regional plan.

After months of debate, in 1982 the revamped TRPA's governing body approved stringent threshold standards for water and air quality, soil conservation, vegetation, noise, wildlife, fisheries, recreation, and scenic resources. The compact defined environmental threshold carrying capacity as "an environmental standard necessary to maintain a significant scenic, recreational, educational, scientific, or natural value of the region or maintain public health and safety within the region."[1]

Most important, the water quality threshold called for a 25 percent reduction of algae-producing nutrients below the annual average between 1973 and 1981. This signaled a long-term commitment to stabilize and reverse the downward trend of Tahoe's water quality. The Tahoe Research Group, Lake Tahoe Interagency Monitoring Program, and U.S. Geological Survey provided the scientific data needed for monitoring water quality.

Nevada accepted the strict standards in exchange for a guarantee that development of single-family house construction could continue on the Nevada side, with a case-by-case review of environmentally sensitive lots. Implementation of the new standards awaited approval of amendments to the regional plan.

Reaching agreement on an amended regional plan proved difficult, especially between environmental advocates of the League to Save Lake Tahoe and private property interests represented by the Tahoe-Sierra Preservation Council. Different plans allowed wide variations in the number of new homes to be constructed, including a proposal to double the basin's population by the early twenty-first century. In 1984, following months in which a TRPA-imposed moratorium blocked construction in the basin, the TRPA's governing body finally approved its amended plan. It called for a maximum of six hundred new homes annually for the next three years.

Soon thereafter, the California attorney general and the league filed legal suits claiming the plan did not protect the environmental quality of Lake Tahoe as provided under the TRPA compact. Federal District Court judge Edward J. Garcia, concluding that Tahoe faced the danger of "irreparable harm," issued an injunction in 1984 that blocked nearly all construction pending approval of an amended regional plan and ordinances conforming to the TRPA compact. The TRPA faced gridlock, and Nevada threatened to withdraw from the agency. If the agency failed, two alternatives appeared likely: local government would regain dominance of decision making within the basin, or the federal government would establish a Lake Tahoe scenic or recreational area. Either option would have been met with a storm of protest.

The preservation council opposed Garcia's ruling and argued that building restrictions constituted an illegal "taking" of property without compensation. As the president of the council pondered, "Our question is whether you are really going to solve anything by taking these lots out of the market, or is it just another ivory tower concept of the squirrel-and-pine-cone crowd?"[2]

When local government and business leaders asked the Urban Land Institute to evaluate land-use planning at Tahoe, the chairman of the institute's panel commented, "Never have I seen so much agreement on what a place should be like and so much polarization about how to get on with it."[3] To the surprise of many local leaders, the panel concluded that the TRPA remained the agency best suited to finding a regional solution to Tahoe's environmental and developmental problems.

At this juncture, Bill Morgan became executive director of the TRPA. He had served ten years as forest supervisor of the Forest Service's Lake Tahoe Basin Management Unit. On taking office, he found a dwindling staff, litigation, a shaky budget, lack of public support, and the possible withdrawal of Nevada from the bistate agency. In addition, Tahoans were at each other's throats: "To environmentalists, developers didn't care that a place of unsurpassable beauty was being wrecked in a myopic, greedy pursuit of quick cash." To many local residents and property rights advocates, the environmentalists didn't care about people's livelihoods or investments and instead wanted "to crush all opposition under a tyrannical, monomaniacal drive to preserve the lake, the cost be damned."[4]

Morgan initiated a novel strategy of consensus negotiations among more than twenty warring factions, representing interests as varied as the Gaming Alliance and the League to Save Lake Tahoe. To aid the discussions, he hired a trained facilitator, Geoffrey H. Ball. As the *Los Angeles Times* described it, "Armed with multicolored marking pens, sheets of butcher paper and a pleasant, even-tempered demeanor, Ball directed scores of negotiating sessions, marking down each argument, starring each concession, coaxing the combatants back to the table when tempers flared."[5] As one participant reported, "Attitudes slowly changed. Provisional agreements emerged. Delicately balanced treaties were constructed. Guidelines for new ordinances were worked out, and finally agreed to."[6] Morgan kept the process alive and supported a middle ground. He believed that the major issue dividing people within the basin was that of equity for property owners and the need to protect environmental quality. "I've always felt that if we want a healthy environment," he stated, "we need a healthy economy because it costs money to fix things in the environment. And without the healthy environment, there would be no economy."[7]

In early 1986 the negotiating group forwarded several recommendations to the TRPA. They agreed that growth should be sharply restricted until past environmental damage was corrected, communities within the basin should establish their own development and environmental goals in relation to the TRPA's long-range plan, the economic consequences of environmental controls should be determined, and the feasibility of building on vacant lots should be evaluated.

By the summer of 1987, the governing body of the TRPA had unanimously adopted a new regional land-use plan to guide environmental protection and development within the Tahoe Basin for the next twenty years. A representative of California's attorney general's office commented, "The new plan balances reasonable growth with the need to control pollution."[8] The plan halved construction permitted under the 1984 plan, allowing only three hundred new single-family homes annually, and limited commercial development to no more than 400,000 square feet in the next decade.

The agreement resulted in Judge Garcia's dismissal of the injunction that had blocked almost all new construction in the basin and had contributed to the economic doldrums that gripped basin businesses in the mid-1980s. The plan provided an innovative Individual Parcel Evaluation System (IPES) for ranking each of the approximately 17,000 residential lots to determine its environmental suitability for development. IPES, which superseded the less flexible Bailey system, was based on such factors as the erosion hazard of the site, the ability of the site to revegetate, and the condition of the watershed. Owners of property deemed unbuildable, such as lots in stream environment zones, could sell their property at fair market value to state or federal agencies. Many prospective sellers, however, contested the price offered to them, arguing that land appraisals failed to recognize the development value of their properties. Those who wished to develop their property had the option to purchase additional property for preservation or foster environmental restoration in order to enhance their ranking for a building permit. The TRPA provided a set of implementing ordinances and over 170 plan area statements to adapt the general plan to the needs of individual neighborhoods.

Shortly thereafter, under section 208 of the federal Clean Water Act, the TRPA amended its *Water Quality Management Plan for the Lake Tahoe Region* to make it consistent with and allow full implementation of the 1987 regional plan. The changes provided more flexibility in managing land use and provided stronger means to improve water quality. In particular, the 208 plan incorporated the new IPES system for evaluating privately owned lots and new policies to protect stream environment zones and regulate land coverage. Ongoing evaluation of water quality could trigger adjustments in the plan as needed to ensure attainment and maintenance of thresholds and standards. Called a "milestone" upon its completion, the TRPA's 208 plan depended on finding close to $300 million for watershed protection projects—a tall order.

Approval of the 208 plan, with its impressive price tag, reflected the magnitude of the problem. As Charles Goldman, the "father" of Lake Tahoe ecological research, explained, most of the algal growth resulted from nonpoint sources "such as disturbed soils, enhanced runoff over impervious surfaces, air pollution, fertilizer applications, and the destruction of natural vegetation and wetlands."[9] Goldman and the Tahoe Research Group theorized that pollutants, especially since urbanization, had accumulated at the bottom of Lake Tahoe in a "nutrient sink." With the mixing of the lake's deep and shallow waters, nutrients came to the surface. Reducing the storehouse of nutrients on the lake's bottom would be a long-term endeavor.

Goldman also explained that algae in Tahoe's waters had become "increasingly sensitive to the addition of phosphorus and trace metals." Whereas nitrogen posed the main contaminant from airborne nutrients, phosphorus proved a major contaminant in stream run-off into the lake. Reducing soil erosion from land disturbances would significantly lower the amount of particulate sediments that transported the phosphorus into Tahoe. Much could be accomplished simply by restoring wetlands that allowed bacterial processes to convert nitrogen compounds into harmless nitrogen gases and intercepted most phosphorus-laden contaminants in sediments before they could enter the lake's water. Nature, left in a healthy state, provided many free ecological services.

As scientist and author Leo Poppoff summarized, researchers continued to study the decline in Tahoe's water quality and to propose solutions to the problem. In the 1960s sewage had been regarded as the primary source of the decline. Then disturbance of Tahoe's watershed became the key factor, followed by discovery of pollutants from the atmosphere. Next, nutrient cycling within the lake drew attention, as well as nutrient-rich groundwater flowing into Tahoe. Finally, in the 1990s scientists recognized that algae growth had changed over the years, feeding first on nitrogen and more recently on phosphorus. Clearly, scientific research remained a key to solving Tahoe's environmental problems.[10]

Forest Health and the U.S. Forest Service

In preparing a land management plan for the LTBMU, the Forest Service had its own concerns: how did Forest Service management affect water quality, what kinds and amounts of outdoor recreation should be provided on national forest land, what degree of resource use was appropriate given national demand, and how should roadless and wilderness areas be managed? The Forest Service faced difficult decisions on how best to balance protection of the land with recreational, resource, and other uses.

In its *Land and Resource Management Plan* (1988), carefully coordinated with the TRPA's regional plan, the Forest Service envisaged the basin's forests in the year 2030. There would be more recreational facilities near existing developed areas. The forest would be healthier and more diverse as a result of active forest management. Environmental thresholds would be achieved, damaged watersheds restored, and water and air quality standards attained and maintained. As Forest Supervisor Bob Harris summarized, "The new plan suits the special nature of the Lake Tahoe Basin. It emphasizes environmental protection and recreation opportunities while providing for modest levels of other resource uses. Like previous plans, the new plan continues to place highest priority on preventing further impacts to water quality and restoring disturbed watersheds."[11] Critics questioned how the Forest Service could provide increased recreational opportunities and continue other resource uses and still meet its environmental goals.

Unfortunately, the forests of Tahoe faced a crisis caused by an extended drought. In 1991 the Forest Service reported 300 million board feet of dead timber within the basin. Probably 25 percent of Tahoe's forest had died—as much as half in some areas. In 1992 a Forest Health Consensus Group formed to encourage a dialogue on possible solutions and make recommendations to the TRPA. At first, participants, citizens, and members of agencies could hardly tolerate contrary views. But like other consensus groups at Tahoe, they came to accept their diversity, held monthly meetings, and kept in touch with many more people via mail.

Early on, the group agreed that a healthy forest depended on "healthy, diverse communities of plants, animals, and fish." The group adopted "ecosystem management" as its guiding principle. These ideas emanated from the writings of American forester and environmentalist Aldo Leopold, who defined land health as "the capacity of the land for self-renewal" and conservation as "our effort to understand and preserve this capacity."[12]

According to a recent ecosystem study at Tahoe, the "challenge of ecosystem management is to sustain systems that are diverse, productive, resistant to short-term stress, and able to respond in a healthy way to long-term change."[13] To achieve such goals depends in part on understanding the ecological role of those who came before, including the Washoes and nineteenth-century Euro-Americans. The latter, in particular, caused disturbances in wild plant populations, the formation and character of soils, and even short-term climate—disturbances not yet fully understood.

The Forest Health group wished to return to forest conditions similar to those that existed before Euro-Americans arrived in the mid-1800s. In brief, they favored the broad forest vegetation types that they believed once predominated. A member of the group noted, "Evidence indicates that in many parts of the Tahoe Basin forests, large mature trees were widely spaced and intermixed with individual trees of various ages. The forest floor, too, was more open, with less brush and fewer downed trees to impede walking. In many cases, the forest floor was opened up by the relatively frequent low intensity 'surface fires' that didn't destroy the forest itself."[14] These open spaces filled with grasses, wildflowers, and shrubs added to the variety of habitats needed to support diverse species of wildlife.

Members of the group blamed current problems on mismanagement of the forest. Loggers had cut accessible sugar, Jeffrey, and yellow pines, leaving white fir trees to reseed the cutover lands. The dense, uniformly aged forest that regrew, protected for decades from fire, neared the end of its natural life cycle in the 1980s, dying from drought and devoured by "nature's loggers," the fir engraver beetle. The beetles normally prey on the relatively few weak trees in the forest, but now they ravage entire stands of firs.

Under natural circumstances, frequent fires clear out underbrush and leave a more varied forest, less susceptible to the impact of disease, insects, drought, and fire. Now, however, the dieback has created a severe fire hazard in which any small fire can turn into an unstoppable firestorm, destroying the vegetative ground cover and un-leashing massive soil erosion into the lake.

Homeowners and business people have called for fire protection. Tahoe Re-Green, established in 1995, has aided efforts to remove dis-eased, dead, and dying trees within and next to residential and com-mercial subdivisions. This cooperative partnership of over twenty government and private agencies provides information and advice to private property owners who request it. Property owners participate voluntarily, shouldering the expense of tree removal on private lands.

The Forest Service has entered into contracts with lumber com-panies for salvage sales of timber. The lumber companies take out dead timber as long as they can cut enough live timber to make the operation profitable. The service uses the revenue for removing log-ging slash, reseeding, erosion control, and other needed work. As Forest Supervisor Bob Harris explained, "The marketing of timber is the basis upon which revenues are generated to get other work ac-complished on the ground."[15] The Forest Service wishes to reduce the chance of devastating fires and enhance its ability to keep the forest healthy.

Some environmentalists, suspicious of the traditional penchant of the Forest Service for logging, have criticized the timber salvage oper-ation, calling it a "subterfuge" to cut old growth. They point to miles of logging roads, soil erosion, and removal of nutrients needed by the forest. Yet so far they have not offered a realistic cost-effective solu-tion to the fire danger except to propose controlled burning and the creation of buffer zones around residential and business zones. Large-scale logging proceeds.

Controlled burning, however desirable, cannot continue on a large scale without first thinning the forest and reducing fuel that could cause a conflagration. A serious financial gap exists between the funds needed by the Forest Service and the bids provided by lum-ber companies willing to undertake salvage logging. Under this lim-itation, the service has done the best it can to reduce the fire danger while working toward the long-term health of the forest.

Public Land Acquisition

Land regulation and planning alone could not save Lake Tahoe from environmental degradation, particularly since thousands of privately owned lots remained ready for development. A TRPA official commented early on that the agency "saw the increase of public lands as the surest way to help ensure environmental control at Lake Tahoe."[16]

Public landownership had a long history at Tahoe as the entire basin originally was part of the public domain. Then, especially after the discovery of the Comstock Lode, farmers and livestock grazers, railroad and logging companies, and tourist-oriented businesses acquired lands in the basin under generous governmental land laws and grants. With the end of the logging era, individual families purchased lots for summer homes, and small businesses appeared along the lakeshore.

Nevertheless, much of the mountainous and forested land away from the shore remained in federal ownership, and Congress began a shift in policy to retain what was left of the public domain for both utilitarian and aesthetic purposes. Acts of Congress and presidential proclamations provided protection for selected tracts of land in the basin, starting with the Lake Tahoe Forest Reserve in 1899. The Forest Service made land exchanges and purchases to add land to the national forests in the basin in the decades that followed. California and Nevada obtained scenic lands for state parks, including prized property along the shores of the lake. Thus, by the early 1970s, agencies of the federal and state governments owned more than 70 percent of the land in the basin, a total that reached 85 percent in the next two decades.

Success of planning efforts and the TRPA's regional plan depended in part on equitable treatment of landowners. Land subdivision, particularly on the California side of the lake, had resulted in thousands of privately owned lots. Owners of these properties, who paid yearly taxes, dreamed of building a summer home, a permanent residence, or a small business. They were outraged when government agencies in the 1970s restricted their freedom to use their property. Then the TRPA, in its revised 1980 compact, limited construction of new homes and commercial development until environmental threshold carrying capacities could be established.

Support for public purchase of these properties, especially in stream environment zones, had grown steadily in the course of the tumultuous debates over land regulation in the 1970s. The TRPA, EPA, Department of the Interior, Western Federal Regional Council, California State Water Resources Control Board, and many other public and private interests supported land acquisition to complement efforts to regulate land use. The Forest Service had accelerated its efforts after Congress passed the Land and Water Conservation Fund Act (1964). It purchased whatever lands became available, especially large tracts that might otherwise have been used for major development projects. In the early 1980s the sites of the proposed Hotel Oliver and Tahoe Palace casinos were purchased to prevent their development. The Forest Service paid a hefty $11.5 million for the latter site. But the acquisition of thousands of small, privately owned lots, a key to Tahoe's environmental future, remained neglected.

To solve this problem, in the early 1980s, Congress and the legislatures of California and Nevada launched three major public land acquisition programs for the Tahoe Basin. Congress approved the Santini-Burton Act (1980), which authorized over $100 million to buy environmentally sensitive land at Tahoe. Over time, these funds were supplemented by an equal amount of funds from the General Fund and other funding sources (including $10 million from Proposition 204 approved by voters in 1996) to implement a comprehensive set of acquisition and site improvement programs. Two years later, California voters approved the Lake Tahoe Acquisitions Bond Act, authorizing $85 million in bonds to purchase lands on the California side of the basin. Finally, in 1986 Nevadans passed the Nevada Tahoe Basin Act, providing $31 million "to preserve the resources and natural beauty" and finance erosion control. (Voters later approved an additional thirty-million-dollar bond act in 1996 for soil erosion control.) These actions represented major steps toward removing environmentally sensitive lands from development and protecting the water quality of Lake Tahoe. The legislation also helped reduce tension between local governments and Tahoe's regulatory agencies, aiding future cooperation in pursuit of environmental goals.

The Santini-Burton Act funded purchase of small lots, something previously not feasible on a large scale. Revenue came from sale to private developers of Bureau of Land Management lands near Las Vegas. The Forest Service, which administered the program, emphasized the purchase of lots in the Tahoe Basin that would be most susceptible to environmental damage if developed. An author in the *California Journal* commented, "It was an ingenious tradeoff—a concession to the Sagebrush Rebellion through the opening of federal lands around Las Vegas in exchange for a greater measure of protection for Tahoe."[17]

Following approval of the Lake Tahoe Acquisitions Bond Act, a commission delegated broad powers to the California Tahoe Conservancy, including purchase of private lands on the California side of the basin. The conservancy explained its diverse activities: "We are implementing programs to protect the natural environment through the acquisition and preservation of environmentally sensitive lands, the implementation of soil erosion control projects, and the transfer of development rights from more sensitive properties to less sensitive ones; to provide new and expanded public access and recreation opportunities; to preserve and restore wildlife habitat; and to manage acquired lands."[18] This broad-based program rested on noncoercive "willing seller" and voluntary methods and close cooperation with federal, regional, state, and local agencies and nonprofit organizations.

During its first twelve years, the conservancy authorized spending over $150 million for the acquisition of "more than 5,450 parcels and the construction of more than 325 site improvement projects in support of its programs."[19] By the early 1990s, in cooperation with the U.S. Forest Service and other public agencies, the conservancy had authorized purchase of nearly two thirds of California lots identified as environmentally sensitive.

Initially, the conservancy's highest priority was acquisition of environmentally sensitive lands, such as steep, erodible slopes and marsh, meadow, and riparian areas vital for settling sediments and capturing nutrients that would pollute the lake. With the passage of time, the conservancy spent most of its funds on "restoring the landscape and wildlife habitat and providing facilities for visitors."[20]

Several factors contributed to the growing emphasis on repair and restoration of damaged lands. Extensive land acquisition provided abundant opportunities for restoration. Achieving environmental thresholds depended on successful site improvement programs. Attaining economic objectives depended on improved environmental quality. Local government and interest groups helped fund efforts to protect the basin's ecosystem and redevelop its economic base.

Rather than establish a new agency such as the California Tahoe Conservancy, Nevada placed its land acquisition program under the administration of the existing Division of State Lands. Under stipulations of its bond act, Nevada paid generously for Tahoe lands. Because of limited funding, the state focused on acquiring environmentally sensitive lands rather than working toward the kind of broader environmental goals pursued in California. Nevada's acquisition program, like those in California, proved successful.

Private Property Rights

However, a number of people sued the TRPA over private property rights. One case, *Kelly v. TRPA*, became the focal point of legal battles. William Code Kelly had bought thirty-nine undeveloped lots at Glenbrook, most on lands considered high hazard under the TRPA's classification system. Nevertheless, he gained a permit from the Douglas County Board of County Commissioners to proceed with development. Under TRPA's dual majority voting scheme of the 1970s, California could not block Kelly's proposed subdivision. The TRPA filed suit in 1975 to annul the Douglas County permit.

Under the amended TRPA compact in 1980 and subsequent new regional plans and ordinances, the TRPA adopted environmental thresholds in order to protect the lake. The TRPA now required a

case-by-case review of single family lots under the IPES. During an
IPES appeal process, Kelly gained approval of development of most of
his lots. Still, he filed suit in 1987 against the TRPA and the states of
Nevada and California. After delays, the Kelly case proceeded to trial
in 1990 and eventually reached the supreme court of Nevada. If Kelly
won, any other property owner in similar circumstances could develop his or her property.

Eventually, in 1993 Nevada's supreme court upheld a district
court ruling that TRPA regulations advanced a legitimate government
interest, the protection of the Lake Tahoe Basin—"a national treasure." It also ruled that Kelly had not been deprived of "all economically viable use" of his property. In fact, he had reaped a substantial
profit, receiving approximately $5.6 million from prior sale of most
of his lots. Further, the supreme court upheld the district court's conclusion that TRPA's action aided Kelly's lots, for the despoliation of
Tahoe would diminish the value of all privately owned lots. In a
unanimous ruling, the supreme court stated, "The Lake Tahoe Basin
appears to be in an environmental tailspin which will eventually destroy it permanently unless preventative measures can be implemented and enforced immediately."[21]

In another important legal action, several hundred owners of undeveloped lots joined with the Tahoe Sierra Preservation Council to
bring legal suits against the TRPA, challenging ordinances, regulations, and prohibitions against development of their properties.
Their original complaints, filed in 1984, sought compensation for the
taking of their property. By 1997, when the case reappeared in a district court, the majority of the original property owners had either
sold their lots under government purchase programs or been granted
building permits. Still, the case had serious implications. If the plain-
tiffs won damages, given the many years in which interest payments
would accrue, the penalties could be enormous. No one knew if the
TRPA could weather such a financial storm or what the impact would
be on its regulatory authority and the future of development within
the Tahoe Basin. Lawsuits continued as a worrisome thorn in the
sides of planners and regulators.

Economic Concerns and Urban Redevelopment

Debate continued over how best to restore Tahoe's environmental quality and provide the basin with a stable economy. These goals went hand in hand. As historian C. Elizabeth Raymond noted, "If Tahoe no longer offers visitors the chance to experience untrammeled nature, or some reasonable facsimile thereof, then all the recreational variety offered by casinos and ski runs may be insufficient to sustain its tourist economy."[22]

Local governments could not bear the cost of remedial environmental action without a sound economy, and local businesses and residents were reluctant to make the sacrifices necessary to attain environmental quality without consideration of their economic needs. According to one observer, the "painful, tedious negotiations in the mid-1980s brought forth a massive, highly experimental set of plans to strike a balance between use of the environment and its protection."[23] No one knew if the experiment would work.

El Dorado County Supervisor John Cefalu expressed the views of many local business interests in the 1980s when he stated, "Regional government controls have crippled Lake Tahoe's economic development." Contractors had left the area, and with them "construction laborers, craftsmen, tradespeople and related businesses."[24] The population of South Lake Tahoe grew less than 1 percent in the decade. At the same time, traffic congestion, drugs, crime, and a shortage of low-cost housing continued to plague the community. Tourism suffered in the face of crowded streets, strip development, and insufficient recreational opportunities. Tahoe's economy stood at a standstill.

In response, the city of South Lake Tahoe initiated a major redevelopment plan that would remove nine hundred old motel rooms and increase open space near Stateline. While some argued that the small-town atmosphere at Tahoe was being sacrificed to high-price, upscale accommodations for the wealthy, nearly two thirds of those polled at South Lake Tahoe approved of the proposed redevelopment program. Many believed that deluxe resorts offered the best opportunity for Tahoe's economic recovery and long-term prosperity.

Embassy Suites Hotel, which opened at the end of 1991, was the initial project in south Tahoe's major redevelopment along Highway 50 from Stateline to just west of Ski Run Boulevard. The Embassy Suites, a seventy-five-million-dollar resort (not to be confused with the Embassy Vacation Resort), the first completed in the area in ten years, was given approval only after meeting strict requirements. Developers had to arrange for removal of 524 older nearby motel rooms before constructing 400 new luxury rooms. As a promotion and marketing manager at Tahoe stated, "It's the first redevelopment program in California history that actually takes out more than it puts in."[25] Planners hope that demolition of the old resorts will reduce air pollution caused by growing numbers of automobiles and provide lands for parks and wetlands to aid water quality in the basin. Underground parking has reduced land coverage and helps check runoff of contaminated storm water from oil drippings from vehicles. The builders conformed to regulations that determined the height of the building, the exterior design, and the colors used. Guestrooms have low-flow toilets and showerheads, a recirculating hot water system eliminates reheating, heavy insulation and double-paned windows conserve energy. The resort cleans its own water before percolating it back into the groundwater. All this added to the cost of construction and ultimately to the cost to the consumer.

A minority of Tahoans have debated the wisdom of constructing luxury resorts. Reporter Kevin Roderick remarked, "One wing of local opinion wants to remake the basin as a world destination resort, with luxury hotels, a busy jetport and fashionable boutiques."[26] It hopes to lure conventions, Japanese skiers, wealthy Texas tourists, and others who would come for a week and spend a lot of money. Another group stresses that nine million people live within a four-hour drive of the lake and that local tourism will inevitably continue to dominate the lake's economy, adding to the traffic congestion and pollution. This contingent thinks that protection of the lake depends less on construction of luxury hotels and more on continued efforts to block new casinos, defeat proposals for freeways, and check construction of new homes.

Community Planning and Cooperation

The consensus building in the mid-1980s that led to the adoption of a revised TRPA regional plan provided opportunities for collaboration among diverse interest groups that had formerly been at loggerheads. Representatives of the Heavenly Ski Resort, the gaming industry, the League to Save Lake Tahoe, and the Tahoe Sierra Preservation Council—the so-called unholy alliance—recognized the advantage of sharing information and seeking common goals. In 1989 this unlikely foursome formed the first of several new collaborative groups, the Tahoe Transportation Coalition. They pondered why environmental quality had not improved and why Tahoe's economy had stagnated in recent years.

At north Tahoe, community planning was already under way. Citizens in Tahoe City and neighboring communities felt disadvantaged, cut off from the county seat in Auburn, which paid most attention to the exploding population in the west county foothills. A proposal to incorporate the urbanized zone between Tahoma and Kings Beach failed from lack of interest. The fast-growing community of Truckee, north of the Tahoe Basin, incorporated in the early 1990s and had a better chance to chart its own course.

In the summer of 1989 a nine-member team of outside experts, the Rural/Urban Design Assistance Team, came to north Tahoe. After an intense four-day visit, the team advised north Tahoans to pool their resources, centralize many services, and coordinate land-use decisions to attain their goals. These goals included commanding a fair share of available governmental resources, providing for expanding numbers of visitors, creating a sense of community, and furnishing "affordable, comprehensive and coordinated transportation."[27] Soon thereafter, a meeting on the north shore led to the formation of the Tahoe Truckee Transportation Management Association. Citizens

of Truckee, Squaw Valley, and north Tahoe described areawide traffic problems and proposed pulling together in a "cohesive regional
entity." In 1991 a coalition of twelve private and public agencies
sponsored the Tahoe Transportation Summit. Its report summarized
the views of many in attendance: "Tahoe is clearly in transition—in
transition from a collection of individual interests plagued by mental
gridlock and bureaucratic malaise to a community empowered to
carry out its plan based on a shared vision."[28]

While Tahoe City's General Plan became one of the first community plans accepted by the TRPA, north Tahoe lacked the political and
financial resources needed for such major redevelopment as a bypass
road around Tahoe City. Local fears and special interests prevailed.
Tahoe City proceeded with an Urban Improvement Project that included improved collection and treatment of run-off water, construction of parking lots, additional sidewalks and gutters, and beautifica-
tion of the business district. Kings Beach, which served as a low-cost
housing area for service workers at north shore casinos and businesses at Incline, opened a public lakefront recreation center, a cen-
terpiece for this culturally diverse community. Incline retained its po-
sition as a wealthy enclave that looked after its own interests. The
north shore remained divided.

When the TRPA provided a five-year evaluation of its performance
in 1991, a shortage of reliable economic information was painfully
evident. As a result, an Economic Round Table met for monthly discussions. Participants wished to end the bickering, accusations, and
lawsuits that had hampered constructive community action for so
long. The discussions led to formation of the Tahoe Truckee Regional Economic Coalition (TTREC), an alliance of public and private
entities formed "to promote a healthy economy, improve quality of
life and integrate the goals of economic health and environmental
enhancement."[29]

The TTREC studied issues related to a diverse and growing resident
population that now exceeded 60,000 in the Tahoe Basin. Over
200,000 tourists visited on a peak summer weekend, to be served by
a growing minority-based labor force. In 1990 minorities repre-

sented 25 percent of the population in South Lake Tahoe and over 30 percent in Kings Beach on the north shore.

The Tahoe Coalition of Recreation Providers (TCORP) pursued a course similar to that of the TTREC, recognizing that Tahoe's billion-dollar economy depended on the protection of the quality of Tahoe's natural environment and the recreational opportunities it provided. The TCORP promoted regional coordination and cooperation and became a clearinghouse for information between recreation providers and the public and private sectors. Further, in 1994 the Tahoe Center for a Sustainable Future was established to gather information and educate and assist those who worked toward environmental protection and sustainable development in the basin.

Not all groups focused on local economics and the environment. The Tahoe-Baikal Institute had international connections. The Resources Agency of California and officials in Siberia signed a memorandum of understanding in 1990 establishing an exchange program for students and scientists working at Tahoe and at Lake Baikal, the largest and deepest freshwater lake in the world. Study groups visited their counterparts abroad, sharing information and points of view. As part of this exchange, native groups around Lake Baikal actively interacted with the Washoes to find means to maintain native ways and regain traditional territories.

Still other groups focused on specific tasks. The Tahoe Rim Trail Fund, a nonprofit and largely volunteer organization formed in 1983, wished to plan, construct, and maintain a 150-mile trail along the ridgeline surrounding Lake Tahoe. Working closely with the Forest Service and the Nevada Division of State Parks, it raised funds and trained trail crews. Anyone can "adopt" a mile of trail for a contribution of $5,000. The trail, including nearly 50 miles of the existing Pacific Coast Trail, is nearing completion.

Other volunteers focused on restoring the Tallac Historic Site. Some of the oldest and finest estates on the south shore, originally owned by the Baldwin, Pope, and Heller families, had faced decay and demolition when the Forest Service purchased the properties in the 1960s and 1970s. Because of lack of funds, the service depended largely on donations and volunteers to help save these properties. Today, this 150-acre site attracts tens of thousands of visitors each summer.

These and other collaborative groups have worked in a growing spirit of cooperation and recognition that the environmental and economic needs of Tahoe go hand in hand. They attempt to reduce onerous regulations where possible and to provide avenues for positive community action. As a group of scientists and public policy experts noted, this recognition rested on a "strong public/private sector commitment to redevelopment and restoration within the Basin as a means of achieving the environmental thresholds, regional planning goals, and economic development objectives."[30] The planning and completion of environmental restoration projects has become a new base for many local contractors and consultants, encouraging local support of such projects.

Since transportation was a shared concern, it provided a rallying point for community action. Under its compact, the TRPA had to develop an integrated regional transportation plan. It established the Tahoe Transportation District to implement its plans and programs. The TRPA was also mandated to maintain federal, state, and local threshold standards for air quality. Five air pollutants in the basin were of particular concern: carbon monoxide, ozone, oxides of nitrogen, coarse particulates, and fine particulates. While some of Tahoe's air pollution came from the Sacramento Valley and beyond, especially during the summer, local sources such as automobile exhaust, dust, wood smoke, and terpenes (oily vapors from wood and trees) reduced visibility and compromised air quality.

The TRPA's transportation and air quality goals concentrate on protecting the carrying capacity of the land in the Tahoe Basin in relation to its ability to tolerate use without sustaining permanent damage. The agency set a goal of reducing total vehicle miles driven in the basin to 10 percent below the level of 1981. The key to achieving this goal is reducing dependency on automobiles. The TRPA has pursued development of public transit by bus and trolley, shuttle services and ride-sharing facilities, increased air and water transportation, completion of a Lake Tahoe Bikeway and the Tahoe Rim Trail, sidewalks for pedestrians, and other alternatives to the automobile.

Community-based transportation management associations, established on the north and south shores, have spearheaded local implementation of transportation improvement projects. Even discussion of a controversial proposal for a basin user fee to help pay for improved public transportation has resurfaced from time to time.

Tahoe, the Sierra Nevada, and Bioregionalism

By the early 1990s, discussions on the entire bioregion of the Sierra Nevada posed new ideas for planners at Tahoe. Tom Knudson wrote a Pulitzer Prize–winning series on the Sierra for the *Sacramento Bee* that appeared in the summer of 1991 and triggered a lively debate. Knudson exposed such problems as wildlife habitats disturbed by overgrazing, overharvesting of timber, traffic congestion, smog, toxic residues from mining activity, overpopulation, and growing pressures on recreational resources. A few months later, CNN aired a five-part news special, "Sierra under Siege," in which Tahoe shared top billing with Yosemite, Sequoia, Kings Canyon, and Mammoth. The Sierra Nevada, including its western foothills, had a growing population of 800,000, which some projected would double in twenty years. Since California's population threatened to surpass 40 million by the year 2010, no one doubted that the Sierra would face increased demand for its resources and as a refuge from urban life.

California State Resources Secretary Douglas Wheeler called for a Sierra Summit that met on a snowy November day in 1991 at Fallen Leaf Lake. Politicians, academics, businessmen, environmentalists, and others initiated a dialogue on how best to counter the environmental degradation that has resulted from overuse of the Sierra. Wheeler emphasized the need to coordinate research programs and improve dissemination of information.

Wheeler wanted management systems for the Sierra to align with the range's natural systems. He called for creation of a bioregional council to provide a common database and to coordinate land-use policies. As one author explained the concept, "In 10 years, each bioregion could have a central office containing all relevant agencies: state, federal and local. People could look together at problems defined by natural boundaries. If a state biologist needed to talk with a federal geologist, he or she would walk down the hall or enter the same computerized database."[31]

Some environmentalists thought the Sierra Summit recommendations too timid, while resource users and local officials feared a state scheme to take control away from local governments. When Wheeler espoused bioregional principles at a public meeting in Bishop, just east of the high Sierra, he met a "tense and frosty silence." The following summer, over four hundred people attended a three-day Sierra Now conference in Sacramento. Participants proposed environmental carrying capacities for the Sierra. Some called for a Sierra regional government, modeled after the TRPA and the California Coastal Commission. Attendees wanted action and created a Sierra Nevada Alliance to implement conference proposals.

No one knows where this activity might lead. Author George Wuerthner presented the idea of a Sierra Nevada Biological Preserve, based on the model of the Adirondack State Park in New York. As Wuerthner explained, "Within the [Adirondack] park boundaries, state lands and private lands are managed for the common goal of preserving the overall wildness, biological integrity and scenic beauty of the region. People do live in the Adirondacks—there are more than 100 communities—and work and play there as well." He noted that "preserving the area's value as a sustainable biological and social community is paramount."[32]

Creation of such a preserve or any form of regional government in the Sierra Nevada had no immediate chance of success because of the heated opposition of local interest groups. In June 1993, Sierra business interests, resource users, and political leaders organized a Sierra Economic Summit. They were concerned about increased government regulations and curtailment of production of lumber and other resources. The following year they formed the Sierra Business Council "to secure and enhance the economic and environmental health of the region for future generations." This organization, which grew to

450 members by 1996, included small shopkeepers as well as major lumber companies and Tahoe casinos.

An increasing number of members of the council recognized that the future well-being of many local economies in the Sierra rested with tourism and recreation, not with extractive industries such as lumber and mining. Thus they called for protection of the natural environment. Steve Teshara, executive director of the Lake Tahoe Gaming Alliance, warned of previous battles between environmentalists and business: "We learned the hard way that fighting doesn't work. And we've recently learned to cooperate and work together. If folks can learn from the lessons and avoid mistakes that we made at Lake Tahoe that would be great."[33]

Both environmentalists and business recognized the need for better information. In response, Congress authorized the Sierra Nevada Ecosystem Project (SNEP). This scientific study was intended to provide comprehensive data to assist Congress and others in making important policy decisions for the future management of the mountain range. According to an author in *Audubon* magazine, the SNEP report noted the dangers "when extractive industries are given free reign, without concern for their ecological consequences, and when too many people crowd in without considering the long-term impact of growth and development."[34] The voluminous SNEP report, published in 1996, provided an abundance of data for consideration. New ideas were aborning.

A Presidential Visit and Plans for the Future

On a Saturday morning in the summer of 1997, a military helicopter descended on the village green at Incline, delivering President Bill Clinton to conduct an Environmental Summit at Lake Tahoe. The official visit, the first by any president in office, focused the nation's attention on the lake, if only for a day. Clinton stated that he wished to highlight the national significance of Lake Tahoe and wanted to show how everybody could work together for a common cause, "recognizing that there cannot be an artificial dividing line between preserving our natural heritage and growing our economy."[35]

The visit was initiated by Nevada senator Harry Reid, who had heard that the first family was considering a summer vacation at Tahoe. Through relentless advocacy by Reid, the vacation idea evolved into an intensive federal study of Tahoe's environmental problems, three high-level workshops led by cabinet secretaries with Tahoe's diverse interest groups, and finally the summit. Those in attendance included the U.S. senators from California and Nevada, the secretaries of agriculture and of the interior, the head of the EPA, and high-ranking officials from the Army Corps of Engineers.

Vice President Al Gore, who arrived the day before the president, took a special interest in the lake, hiking part of the Tallac Trail with a large group of journalists and holding a workshop on the south shore. Together, he and the president took a short ride on the Tahoe Research Group vessel, the *John LeConte*, getting a quick lesson on the lake's water quality. Their instructor, Professor Charles Goldman, commented afterward, "This is the single most important event I've observed in my 40 years at Lake Tahoe. I think it's probably the first time a president has come to save a lake."[36]

The long-term significance of the presidential visit remains to be seen. In the short run, Clinton pledged to double federal spending for the next two years to $50 million and to work with Congress to secure additional funding. He cited twenty-five environmental improvement projects to be tackled immediately, including elimination of many old logging roads, reduction of fire danger through controlled burns, new computer modeling for evaluating Tahoe's water quality, and expansion of the mass transit system. The president also signed an executive order citing national concern for the lake and ordering federal agencies to coordinate their efforts with others working to address Tahoe's environmental and economic concerns.

Critics complained that $50 million was a far cry from the ten-year, 906-million-dollar Environmental Improvement Program hammered out by the TRPA. This blueprint for more than four hundred projects was aimed at achieving environmental thresholds for the basin. The burden of the expense was estimated as follows: $274 million by California, $82 million by Nevada, nearly $300 million by the federal government, over $150 million by private investment, and about $100 million by local jurisdictions.

The call for substantial new funding reflected a growing awareness that land-use planning and regulation alone could not achieve environmental threshold carrying capacities. New strategies were needed to repair damage to the environment and restore the basin's ecosystem to a healthy state.

In the week prior to the presidential visit, the governors of California and Nevada met at the Heavenly Ski Resort to renew formally their states' commitment to restoring Lake Tahoe. Earlier that month, the four legislative leaders of the two states reaffirmed their legislatures' commitment to the principles of the TRPA compact and to securing funds needed to achieve its objectives.

In spite of its critics, the presidential visit represented an important step forward, signaling a renewed federal presence and commitment. The people at Tahoe, in turn, gave something back to the nation. As Vice President Gore noted, "Your cooperation to protect Lake Tahoe is, frankly, an outstanding model for the work we have to do to protect all kinds of national treasures and deal with all kinds of environmental challenges in the new century.[37]

Conclusion

The Lake Tahoe basin has been altered markedly since John Frémont first sighted the lake from a mountain peak in 1844. Although Lake Tahoe itself looks much the same today when seen from such a distance, closer inspection of the lands along its shores reveals the magnitude of human impact. While the Washoes left the land little changed, lumbermen cut most of the accessible timber. Even so, a second growth of timber covered the mountain slopes, and the lake recuperated from most of the damage to the quality and clarity of its water.

During the next fifty years, the Tahoe Basin underwent slow growth as a summer resort. Most people assumed that Tahoe would remain a rustic, quiet, summer retreat. But then a series of events, including the population explosion in California, the completion of improved highways to the basin, the rapid expansion of winter recreation activities, and especially the construction of year-round casino-hotels, combined to produce a rate of urbanization that no one had prepared for or expected.

Here was runaway development with no apparent end in sight. The water of Lake Tahoe was given no hiatus to recover from the onslaught of nutrients from sewage, roads, construction sites, landfills, dredging, and storm runoff. Even when the damage was not visible to the casual observer, anyone accustomed to swimming at Tahoe could not help noticing the steady accumulation of slippery green algae on the once clean rocks along the shoreline.

Fortunately, despite the problems, much has been accomplished to protect the lake and its surroundings. The concerted efforts of many dedicated people and organizations have led to establishment of several beautiful state parks and extensive national forests; curtailment of road and highway construction; prohibition of new casinos; export of sewage from the basin; research and monitoring that yielded an improved understanding of how Tahoe's ecosystem functions; increased understanding of Tahoe's place in the Sierra Nevada ecosystem; greater public awareness and cooperative efforts to find solutions to Tahoe's environmental problems; and expenditure of hundreds of millions of dollars on land acquisition and restoration projects. Acceptance of new TRPA, water quality, and forestry plans have provided an opportunity for further progress.

A group of leading planners and scientists recently sent a report to Congress in which they set forth an assessment of Tahoe's ecosystem.[1] They acknowledge many "lessons" from their studies and efforts to contribute to the long-term health of the Lake Tahoe basin ecosystem:

> It takes time and effort to create a unified vision.
> Litigation is costly.
> Threshold-based planning shows promise for ecosystem management.
> Land acquisition and restoration programs are of great value.
> Redevelopment is a tool.
> Ecological monitoring is costly but extremely valuable.
> Long-term ecological research is valuable.

In addition, the report notes that coalitions, partnerships, and education benefit the community and the ecosystem of which it is a part.

Progress in saving Tahoe, especially since 1980, has "required public support, legislative, judicial, and/or regulatory agency action, the cooperation of all levels of government, the involvement of public and private landowners, the involvement of interest groups, an evolving set of regulatory mechanisms and actions, acquisition and restoration programs, and a high level of collaboration between all players to conserve this ecosystem."[2] Who could blame planners if they felt fatigued by their efforts?

Tahoe's future remains problematic. As limnologist Charles Goldman writes: "Lakes are truly reservoirs of history in that they collect in their waters and sediments an indelible record of whatever has transpired on their watersheds. . . . The effects of what we do or don't do today will be felt for years to come. Tahoe has a long memory."[3]

Notes

Preface

1. U.S. Senate Committee on Public Works, Subcommittee on Air and Water Pollution, Hearings, *Environmental Problems of the Lake Tahoe Basin*, 92d Cong., 2d sess., 21 August 1972, 57.
2. Charles R. Goldman, "Bad News from Lake Tahoe," *Cry California* 3 (winter 1967–68): 12.

1. From Pioneers to Urbanites

1. Susan Lindström, "Lake Tahoe Case Study: Lake Levels," in *Sierra Nevada Ecosystem Project Final Report to Congress: Status of the Sierra Nevada*, Addendum, Wildlands Resources Center Report No. 40 (Davis: University of California Center for Water and Wildland Resources, 1997), 265.
2. Susan Lindström, "Spatial Patterns of Sierra Landscape Change, 1820–1960, Lake Tahoe Basin," draft MS (1995).
3. Jennifer Ragland, "Washoe Home at Last," *Tahoe Daily Tribune*, 27 July 1997.
4. Brevet Col. J. C. Frémont, *The Exploring Expedition to the Rocky Mountains, Oregon and California* (Buffalo NY: Geo. H. Derby, 1852), 334.
5. G. H. G., "Lake Bigler," *Hutchings California Magazine* 2 (September 1857): 107.
6. "Description of Lake Bigler," *Daily Alta California* (San Francisco), 7 July 1859.
7. "A Day on Lake Bigler," *Sacramento Union*, 9 September 1862.
8. Charles H. Shinn, "Report on the Proposed Addition to the Lake Tahoe Forest Reserve, California," 31 October 1902, 54, in Drawer 134, Re-

search Compilation File, Records of the U.S. Forest Service, Record Group 95, National Archives, Washington DC.

9. "Lake Tahoe," *Sacramento Daily Union*, 13 August 1863.

10. E. A. Sterling, "Report on the Forest Condition in the Lake Tahoe Region, California," June 1904, 4, copy in Forest Library, University of California, Berkeley.

11. Quoted in "Mountain Vandalism," *Pacific Coast Wood and Iron* 12 (September 1889): 70.

12. Shinn, "Report," 12.

13. Lake Tahoe Railway and Transportation Company, *Tahoe Tavern, Lake Tahoe, California* [1905?], promotional brochure, copy in Bancroft Library, University of California, Berkeley.

14. A. J. Wells, *Lake Tahoe and the High Sierra* (San Francisco: Southern Pacific, 1906), 9.

15. *Tallac* (n.d.), promotional brochure, copy in Bancroft Library.

16. Wells, *Lake Tahoe*, 2.

17. "Great Project" and "California Will Share Its Scenic Gifts," *San Francisco Call*, 18, 19 May 1912.

18. William D. Rowley, "Reno and the Desert of Buried Hopes," in Wilbur S. Shepperson, ed., *East of Eden, West of Zion: Essays on Nevada* (Reno: University of Nevada Press, 1989), 122.

19. "Tahoe Nightlife," *Tahoe Tattler*, 8 August 1941.

20. "Signs Point to North Shore Boom," *Nevada State Journal*, 22 June 1960.

2.   Parks, Forests, and Water

1. John Muir, "Lake Tahoe in Winter," *Sierra Club Bulletin* 3 (May 1900): 122–23, repr. from the *San Francisco Bulletin*.

2. "Lake Tahoe," *Truckee Tribune*, 7 September 1878.

3. "Report of the Lake Bigler Forestry Commission," in *Appendix to the Journals of the Senate and Assembly in the Twenty-Sixth Session of the Legislature of the State of California*, pt. 5 (Sacramento, 1885), 12.

4. Mills to Binger Hermann, 17 December 1897, Box 151 (Division R, National Forest, Tahoe), Record Group 49, National Archives, Washington DC (hereafter cited as RG 49).

5. "Remonstrance," n.d., Box 151, RG 49.

6. Muir to Newhall, 1 December 1900, Box 151, RG 49.

7. Marsden Manson, "Observations on the Denudation of Vegetation: A Suggested Remedy for California," *Sierra Club Bulletin* 2 (June 1899): 298.

8. California Water and Forest Association, *Should the Forests Be Preserved?* (1903), 6.

9. California Water and Forest Association, *Should the Forests Be Preserved?* 12.

10. *Sacramento Evening Bee*, 9 May 1903.

11. Stewart to the President, 8 October 1903, Box 151, RG 49.

12. Quotations from Toll to Director, 30 April 1932, attached to W. P. Mott, "Proposed Lake Tahoe National Park," 13 December 1935, Box 2951, File 0-51 Tahoe, Central Classified File 1933–49, Proposed National Parks (0-32), Records of the National Park Service, Record Group 79, National Archives, Washington DC.

13. This account of land acquisition is based on [Andrew R. Schmidt], "The Role of the United States Forest Service and Other Federal Agencies in the Lake Tahoe Region," (USDA Forest Service, June 1979), 87–97, copy at USFS headquarters, South Lake Tahoe.

14. *Park, Parkway and Recreational Area Study* (Carson City NV: State Printing Office, 1938), 80.

3. Planning and Growth

1. *Lake Tahoe* [December 1965?], copy in unprocessed file, Nevada Historical Society, Reno.

2. Jeff Brown, "Tahoe Notebook," *Holiday* 38 (December 1965): 78.

3. Raymond F. Smith, "Objectives of a Planning Program at Lake Tahoe," in Lake Tahoe Area Council, *Topic Report no. 7* (June 1960), 3.

4. Robert A. Burco, *Policy and Planning in the Lake Tahoe Basin: The Case of Transportation* (Davis: University of California Institute of Governmental Affairs, 1973), 43.

5. A. W. West and K. M. Mackenthun, *Report on Pollution in the Lake Tahoe Basin, California-Nevada* (Cincinnati: U.S. Department of the Interior, Federal Water Pollution Control Administration, 1966), 38.

6. J. T. Leggett and F. R. McLaren, "The Lake Tahoe Water Quality Problem: History and Prospectus," *California Water Pollution Control Association Bulletin* 6 (October 1969): 6–8.

7. Charles R. Goldman, *Eutrophication of Lake Tahoe Emphasizing Water Quality* (Corvallis OR: U.S. Environmental Protection Agency, 1974), 11.

8. "Z'Berg Opposes Compromise on Tahoe Compact," *Sacramento Bee*, 25 January 1968.

9. Raymond G. Davis, *Regional Government for Lake Tahoe: A Case*

Study (Davis: University of California Institute of Governmental Affairs, 1970), 22–23.

10. Mike Hayden, *Guidebook to the Lake Tahoe Country*, 2 vols. (Los Angeles: Ward Ritchie, 1971), 2:65.

11. William Bronson, "It's About Too Late for Tahoe," *Audubon* 73 (May 1971): 52.

12. Bronson, "It's About Too Late," 77.

13. Bronson, "It's About Too Late," 61.

14. Quoted in Chris Bowman, "Impact of Added Casinos Is Cited," *Sacramento Bee*, 26 January 1977.

15. Oliver Kahle, "An Economic Assessment," *Tahoe Reflections* (November 1974): 6.

16. Gale Cook, "Storm of Emotions Buffet Lake Tahoe," *San Francisco Chronicle*, 23 June 1974.

17. David Johnston, "Building Boom to End at Lake Tahoe," *Los Angeles Times*, 28 March 1977.

18. Quoted in "Building Ban Sought," *Lake Tahoe News*, 23 January 1980.

19. "Casino Fight," *Sacramento Bee*, 18 November 1978.

20. Bob Keely, "Nevada Scene," in Datebook, *San Francisco Chronicle*, 3 February 1980.

21. Western Federal Regional Council, *Lake Tahoe Environmental Assessment*, 192.

22. "Lake Tahoe Tomorrow," California Resources Agency news release, 12 December 1977.

23. USDA Forest Service, California Region, Lake Tahoe Basin Management Unit, *Land Management Plan*, Part 1 (1978), 77.

4.   Seeking New Ground

1. Tahoe Regional Planning Agency, *Draft* 1996 Evaluation Report, 1.

2. Wallace Turner, "Irate Property Owners Fuel Attack on Tahoe Planning Agency," *New York Times*, 10 March 1985.

3. Barbara Ingrum, "Progress at Tahoe," *Urban Land* 44 (November 1986): 13.

4. Jim DiPeso, "TRPA Chief Recounts Achievements," *Tahoe World*, 8 June 1989.

5. Ronald B. Taylor, "Preliminary Tahoe Accord Could See End to Long Battle," *Los Angeles Times*, 20 January 1986.

6. Leo Poppoff, "Bidding a Fond Farewell to TRPA's Bill Morgan," *Tahoe World*, 5 October 1989.

7. Jock Friedly, "TRPA Chief Leaves a Legacy," *Tahoe World*, 3 August 1989.

8. Genevieve Leone, "Tahoe Plan Approved," *Northern California Real Estate Journal*, 17–30 August 1987, 5.

9. Charles Goldman, "Lake Tahoe: Preserving a Fragile Ecosystem," *Environment* 31 (1989): 11.

10. Leo Poppoff, "What Have We Learned about Lake Tahoe So Far?" *Tahoe World*, 7 July 1988.

11. Ken Heiman, "Forest Service Unveils Management Plan for Tahoe," *Tahoe World*, 8 December 1988.

12. Aldo Leopold, *A Sand County Almanac* (New York: Oxford University Press, 1949), 221.

13. Susan Lindström and Sharon Waechter, *North Shore Ecosystems Project Heritage Resource Inventory*, Vol. 1: Report (South Lake Tahoe CA: USDA Forest Service, October 1995), 6.

14. John Cobourn, "Forest Health Consensus Group Looks to the Future," n.d.

15. Andrew O'Hehir, "Should Tahoe Burn," *San Francisco Focus* 42 (1995): 38.

16. Quoted in Richard J. Fink, "Public Land Acquisition for Environmental Protection: Structuring a Program for the Lake Tahoe Basin," *Ecology Law Quarterly* 18 (1991): 513.

17. Leo Rennert, "Burton's Half-Loaf," *California Journal* (January 1981): 35.

18. California Tahoe Conservancy, *Progress Report: 1985–1991*, 30 June 1991, 1.

19. California Tahoe Conservancy, *Progress Report* [1997], 3.

20. California Tahoe Conservancy, *Progress Report* [1997], 3.

21. *William Code Kelly v. TRPA*, Supreme Court of Nevada, filed 8 July 1993, 18.

22. Peter Goin, C. Elizabeth Raymond, and Robert E. Blesse, *Stopping Time: A Rephotographic Survey of Lake Tahoe* (Albuquerque: University of New Mexico Press, 1992), 21.

23. Jim DiPeso, "TRPA Marks 20 Active Years in the Tahoe Basin," *Tahoe World*, 8 June 1989.

24. John Cefalu, "Tahoe's Economic Environment Crippled," *California County* (May–June 1987): 25.

25. Laura Del Rosso, "Embassy Suites' Opening," *Travel Weekly* 50 (December 1991): 49.

26. Kevin Roderick, "Tahoe's Rural Tone in Danger," *Los Angeles Times*, 1 April 1991.

27. Regional/Urban Design Assistance Team, *Accepting Limits and Forging a Vision*, 14–17 July 1989, 25.

28. Leigh, Scott and Cleary, Inc., *Tahoe Transportation Summit: Final Report*, 20 June 1991, 3.

29. "Tahoe Truckee Regional Economic Coalition Mission Statement," n.d.

30. Lindström, "Lake Tahoe Case Study," 242.

31. Paul McHugh, "Reinventing the Map: Bioregionalism—The Grass-Roots Movement that Uses Natural Boundaries," in *This World, San Francisco Chronicle*, 13 September 1992.

32. George Wuerthner, *California's Sierra Nevada* (Helena MT: American and World Geographic Publishing, 1993), 97.

33. "High Country Common Ground," *New York Times*, 30 November 1996.

34. Martin Forstenzer, "What's Wrong in the Sierra?" *Audubon* 99 (March 1997): 14.

35. Faith Bremmer, "Clinton Preaches Cooperation to Save Lake," *Reno Gazette-Journal*, 27 July 1997.

36. Jeff DeLong, "President Receives a Lesson in Biology," *Reno Gazette-Journal*, 27 July 1997.

37. Bremmer, "Clinton Preaches Cooperation."

Conclusion

1. *Sierra Nevada Ecosystem Project Final Report to Congress.*

2. Lindström, "Lake Tahoe Case Study," 217, 256–57.

3. Charles R. Goldman, "Tahoe Water Clarity," *Sunset* 188 (May 1992): 107.

Index